Author

This GCSE guide was written by Kerry Lewis, author of 'Mr Bruff's Guide to Grammar' and 'Mr Bruff's Guide to A' Level English Literature'. Both books have been number one on the Amazon secondary education best seller lists, and the A' level book has also been number one on Amazon's curricula best seller list. Kerry has been a member of the mrbruff.com team since May 2014. You can follow her on Twitter @Mrs_SPaG.

Dedications

Kerry Lewis would like to thank Andrew Simmons for offering his expertise and support with the final draft of this book. She would also like to thank Christina Turner and Sylvie Bartlett-Rawlings for their help with the German and French translations respectively; she has greatly appreciated their bilingual input.

Mr Bruff would like to thank Sunny Ratilal and Sam Perkins, who designed the front cover of this eBook.

Contents

Introduction

Charlotte Brontë was 31 years old when 'Jane Eyre' was published under the male pseudonym of Currer Bell. It was one of the earliest novels written from the perspective of a female, and it became an immediate best seller.

Why was it so popular? First of all, Jane is not the conventionally beautiful heroine. Small, plain Jane is based on a real woman: Charlotte Brontë herself. In a time when women were judged by their looks, many readers—at that time, mainly women read novels—could relate to Jane. Some may also have identified with the novel challenging contemporary beliefs about the role of women, who were restricted by their gender. Of course, it is a wonderful love story, but independently-minded Jane questions the role of a Victorian wife, who becomes the legal property of her husband upon marriage. Defying the stereotype of the passive female, Jane has the self-confidence to be guided by her own ideas about what is right and wrong.

Nearly two hundred years later, readers are still swept into Jane's narrative to share her thoughts and feelings. We are intrigued by the strange laughter in the dark of the night at Thornfield Hall; suspicious of the enigmatic Grace Poole, suspected of setting fire to Mr Rochester's bedclothes; and unnerved by the 'Vampyre' attack on the mysterious Mr Mason. Finally, some of the supernatural events turn out to be real, which makes for an even more thrilling read!

As well as containing lots of analysis of language and form, this GCSE revision guide examines the structure of the novel in a completely new way—Freytag's Pyramid applied to each setting rather than the entire novel. An analysis of context has been blended into themes, to reflect the marks available for context in the GCSE specifications.

It is worth mentioning that, in addition to his wide range of revision guides, Mr Bruff has a flourishing YouTube channel with over one thousand videos focusing on GCSE English language and English literature as well as the A' levels in English literature and language. His videos have been viewed over 11 million times across 198 nations.

I hope you find this revision guide useful!

Kerry Lewis

@Mrs_SPaG

The Author: Charlotte Brontë

Charlotte Brontë (1816-1854) was the third of six children born to the Reverend Patrick Brontë and his wife, Maria. In 1821, the family moved from Thornton (near Bradford in Yorkshire) to Haworth where, a year later, Mrs Brontë died of cancer.

Although Charlotte's aunt helped Patrick to look after the children, he found the strain of raising such a young family difficult. Consequently, in 1824, he sent seven-year-old Charlotte with three of her sisters to a boarding school, the Clergy Daughters' School at Cowan Bridge. This absence of parent figures might be reflected in her novels, as all four of her heroines are orphans. After a year, the two eldest daughters, eleven-year-old Maria and ten-year-old Elizabeth, became seriously ill with tuberculosis. They returned home and shortly died. Worried about the health of his remaining daughters, the Rev. Brontë brought home Charlotte, now eight, and Emily, six.

Charlotte uses the people and conditions of the Clergy Daughters' School as the basis for Lowood School in 'Jane Eyre'. The trauma of losing Helen Burns is based on Charlotte's loss of her sister Maria. Charlotte's cruel teacher Miss Andrews becomes Miss Scatcherd, and the tyrannical head teacher the Rev. Carus Wilson becomes Mr Brocklehurst. There are other parallels too: hardships at both schools included small portions of sometimes spoiled food; insufficient heating; inadequate clothes for the winter; and epidemics of fevers.

We learn in the Lowood chapters that the Victorians believed in the miasma theory, which was the belief that diseases such as typhus were caused by a miasma, or 'bad air' in the form of fog and mist. At Lowood, Jane states that the warm temperatures combine with the school's unhealthy location to create a breeding-ground for typhus—the Victorians were in fact unaware that typhus is spread by body lice and dirty conditions.

In 1826, Mr. Brontë gave his children a box of wooden soldiers. The toys appealed to the imaginations of Branwell, the girls' only brother, Charlotte, Emily, and Ann (the youngest of the children), who created and wrote about an imaginary world called Angria. The literature from this time still survives and is known as Brontë juvenilia.

When she was fifteen, Charlotte attended Roe Head School, which she returned to as a teacher from 1835 to 1838. In the novel 'Jane Eyre', this might be reflected in Jane finishing her education at Lowood School and then staying on as a teacher. A year later, Charlotte worked as governess for the Sidgewick family but, disliking the position, she left after just three months. It was there that one of her pupils threw a Bible at her; this incident might be replicated in chapter 1 of 'Jane Eyre' in which John Reed throws a book at Jane.

Charlotte's distaste for living with another family and earning a living as a governess can be seen in her return to Haworth where she and her sisters decided to establish their own school. To prepare for this, Charlotte and Emily went to Brussels in 1842 to finish their education. Charlotte, after returning home to attend the funeral of her aunt, returned to Brussels alone and stayed until 1844. The influence of her time in abroad can be seen in her novels 'Shirley', with the French-speaking Belgian brother and sister, Robert and Hortense Moore; 'Villette' and 'The Professor', which are set in schools in Belgium; and 'Jane Eyre' with the French dialogue instigated by Adèle.

Back in Haworth, the plans to open a school failed miserably, as no-one responded to the sisters' advertisements. Their literary careers, however, began when Charlotte discovered some poems that Emily had written. This prompted the sisters to self-finance a collection of their poems.

Despite selling just three copies of the poems, the sisters continued to write. It was a decision that they would not regret. Although Charlotte's first novel, 'The Professor', was rejected for publication, her second novel 'Jane Eyre, An Autobiography' became a best seller when it was published in 1847. In the same year, Emily's 'Wuthering Heights', and Ann's 'Agnes Grey' were published.

Charlotte decided to publish under the name of Currer Bell, because she did not want her characters or locations to be recognised by people she knew and she was aware of prejudice against female writers. When she had been teaching at Roe Head School a few years earlier, she had written to the Poet Laureate Robert Southey to ask for his opinion of her talents. He had replied: 'Literature cannot be the business of a woman's life and it ought not to be'. Aware of contemporary prejudice, the sisters chose to publish under male pseudonyms, keeping the initials of their first names. Charlotte, as we have seen, became Currer Bell, Emily was Ellis Bell and Ann was Acton Bell.

In Charlotte's novels, we have fascinating insights into contemporary beliefs and the culture of the time. For instance, in 'Jane Eyre' we learn some of Charlotte's thoughts about the impact of the Industrial Revolution, which profoundly changed the social, economic and indeed the physical landscape of parts of Britain. Manufactured goods created much wealth for the factory owners and, in the novel, we meet Rosamond Oliver's father, who owns a 'needle-factory' and a 'foundry' while his daughter Rosamond is a philanthropist, who gives away money to help others. Although conditions for the workers are not referred to in the novel, Brontë's negative views about the Industrial Revolution are implied in the Moor House chapters.

In chapter 32, for example, Jane muses on how the Industrial Revolution has had a powerful negative effect on art. She states that 'Marmion', a poem of passion and heroism set in the 16th century, written by Sir Walter Scott, is 'one of those genuine productions so often vouchsafed to the fortunate public of those days—the golden age of modern literature'. Scott was a key figure in the Romantic movement, which glorified nature, focused on romance and passion, and had a strong sense of nostalgia. These beliefs are obviously shared by Jane, who implies that the 'golden age of modern literature' is over because of widespread industrialisation, leaving no room for grand gestures of bravery and passion.

Although in Jane's view the Industrial Revolution threatened the artist's place in the world and was a threat to creativity, Jane reassures the reader further on in chapter 32 that 'poetry' and 'genius' 'not only live, but reign and redeem: and without their divine influence spread everywhere, you would be in hell—the hell of your own meanness'.

This passionate outburst suggests that without the divine influence of poetry, we would be in a hell of our own making. To enforce her point, she directly addresses the reader with the use of the second person ('you') and deliberately uses repetition ('hell') and emotive language ('your own meanness'). This is a passionate outburst and, because it has no relevance to the plot, the reader concludes that Jane is voicing Charlotte Brontë's own views.

A further example of how contemporary beliefs found their way into 'Jane Eyre' is the use of phrenology. Phrenology was a pseudo-science, which involved the study of the shape of people's skulls and faces, and Victorians believed that they could use this information to read a person's character type. We see an example of phrenology in the novel when Jane is ill in bed at Moor House. St. John tells his sisters that her 'physiognomy' (facial characteristics) are 'not indicative of vulgarity or degradation'. Another example is when Jane first sees Mr Rochester at Ferndean. She states 'in his countenance, I saw a change: that looked desperate and brooding'. It is obvious that he has physically changed, but she attempts to read his 'countenance' (i.e. face) and deduces that his character has changed as well.

A year after the publication of 'Jane Eyre', Charlotte and Ann went to London (Emily refused to accompany them) to quash a rumour that the three novels were written by the same person. Their publisher George Smith was greatly surprised to learn that they were young women. He coped admirably by introducing them to his mother and taking them to the theatre.

In September of the same year, Branwell, now an alcoholic and opium addict, died from tuberculosis, an infection of the lungs. Three months later, tuberculosis also took Emily and then the following May, Ann.

In 1849, the same year that 'Shirley' was published, George Smith encouraged Brontë to meet her readers. She was extremely shy about speaking to strangers, but she met many great writers of the time, including William Makepeace Thackeray and Elizabeth Gaskell. Gaskell later wrote Charlotte's biography. In 1851, she visited the Great Exhibition and the Crystal Palace in London. In 1853, 'Villette' was published.

In 1854, Charlotte married the Rev. A. B. Nicholls. This was not the first time that he had proposed to her: Rev. Brontë had objected to the match, regarding his famous daughter as too good for the impoverished Irish curate. Her father finally consented to the wedding, however.

Nine months later, the pregnant Charlotte died three weeks before her thirty-ninth birthday. Various causes of death have been cited, including tuberculosis, typhoid, acute morning sickness and pneumonia.

Two years later, her first novel, 'The Professor', was posthumously published. In the same year, Elizabeth Gaskell's biography, 'The Life of Charlotte Brontë' was published.

Significance of the Title

The title page of the first edition, published in 1847, was as follows:

JANE EYRE

An Autobiography

Edited by

CURRER BELL

The title suggests that this is a genuine autobiography that has been edited by the male writer Currer Bell. As we saw in Brontë's biography, this reflects the contemporary prejudice against female writers. The subtitle 'An Autobiography' is deceptive: the novel is actually a fictional autobiography; the modern reader becomes aware, however, that many elements of Brontë's life have been woven into it. The subtitle prepares the reader for the fact that the novel will be narrated in the first person by Jane.

The name 'Jane' has associations with 'plain Jane'. Her simple forename emphasises the difference in status between Jane and the well-bred ladies in the novel, who have higher status names such as Eliza, Georgiana, Blanche and Rosamond. There are also associations with speaking plainly, which is what she does to Mr Rochester.

The surname 'Eyre' has many layers of meaning because it is a homophone. For example, one homophone for 'eyre' is 'heir': the reader learns that this is the story of John Eyre's heir. Another homophone is 'air'. Like a spirit of the air, Jane drifts from one location to the next, looking for her place in the world. Mr Rochester calls Jane a 'fairy', 'sprite' and 'elf', conveying the idea that she is petite and slender. As Jane is a slip of a girl, this adds to the other-worldly imagery and emphasises her position as a free spirit, difficult to catch and hold down. Finally, in medieval times, an eyre was a circuit court held by a judge (a justice in eyre), who travelled from county to county. Jane, like a justice in eyre, travels, and she judges or evaluates everything that she sees. Her sense of justice is particularly strong in the Gateshead and early Lowood chapters when she is surrounded by people who abuse their positions of power. Finally, Jane employs justice to make amends. When she decides to share her inheritance with her Rivers cousins, she states 'justice would be done'.

Form and Genre

'Form' is the shape of a piece of writing; for example, prose, drama and poetry. 'Jane Eyre' is a prose novel, which takes the sub-form of a fictional autobiography (discussed above). The decisions that Brontë made when writing her fictional autobiography have a considerable impact on the ways that we read and interpret the novel.

Decision 1: First Person Narration with an Older Jane Intruding

The story is narrated in the first person ('I'), from the point of view of Jane at each stage of her life. The use of the first person establishes her character, which is introduced to us through themes, and guides our response. Sometimes, an older Jane interrupts. For example, the older Jane says:

> No severe or prolonged bodily illness followed this incident of the red-room; it only gave my nerves a shock of which I feel the reverberation to this day. Yes, Mrs. Reed, to you I owe some fearful pangs of mental suffering, but I ought to forgive you, for you knew not what you did: while rending my heart-strings, you thought you were only uprooting my bad propensities.

When the older Jane says that her nerves are still affected 'to this day', the reader feels sympathy for the younger Jane, as we now appreciate the devastating long-term psychological impact of being locked in the red-room. It is interesting to see the verb 'ought' is used when she says 'I ought to forgive you', implying that she has still not managed to forgive her aunt. This is despite Jane apparently forgiving Mrs Reed on her deathbed: Jane attempted to behave like a good Christian at the time of Mrs Reed's death, but she reveals in her comment that she continues to carry deep psychological scars.

Decision 2: Shift from Past to Present Tense

At the beginning of chapter 11, Jane shifts from the past to the present tense when she describes her surroundings at the George Inn at Millcote: the 'large figured papering on the walls as inn rooms have; such a carpet, such furniture, such ornaments on the mantelpiece, such prints' etc. The present tense and long list slow time down, encouraging the reader to share Jane's observations. (The repetition of 'such' adds rhythm—we can almost imagine Jane being lulled into drowsiness by a warm fire after her long, cold, tiring journey.)

Decision 3: Direct Address

There are many examples of direct address in the novel. After describing the room at the George Inn in chapter 11, for example, Jane directly addresses the reader: 'Reader, though I look comfortably accommodated, I am not very tranquil in my mind.' This signifies a change of mood. The focus switches to Jane's own state of mind, shifting from the external world to her feelings, as we realise that appearances can be deceptive and that she is nervous and worried. The use of direct address and present tense together therefore create tension, as the reader identifies with Jane and shares her 'doubts and fears' about whether she will be collected or not. Structurally, chapter 11 starts with loneliness and fear but ends with happiness and companionship. Therefore, the use of direct address and the present tense at the start of the chapter heightens these contrasts and tensions.

Decision 3: Shift from Present to Past Tense

Once Jane has expressed her fears about not being collected from the George Inn, she continues the narration of her story in the past tense: 'fear with me became predominant when half-an-hour elapsed and still I was alone. I bethought myself to ring the bell.' The final sentence signals a change in mood as she makes an active decision and takes control. Switching from the present to past tense therefore speeds up the narrative.

Decision 4: Deliberately withholding Information from the Reader

We know that the story is narrated by an older Jane who sometimes intrudes herself into the story. She could have revealed much earlier that Mr Rochester was married, but she chooses to withhold this and other information from the reader. This adds tension and captures the reader's imagination: for example, we share the younger Jane's distress when we discover at the same time as her that Mr Rochester is married.

There are many further examples of withholding information to create suspense for the reader. In chapter 36, the reader wants to see Jane quickly reunited with Mr Rochester when she leaves Moor House and arrives at Thornfield Hall, but Brontë deliberately delays a reunion and creates suspense through:

- A description of Jane's goodbyes and her journey to Thornfield Hall.
- Telling a story about a 'mistress asleep on a mossy bank' when all we want to hear about is Thornfield Hall. This also heightens the shock when she sees that the house has burnt down.
- The use of direct speech when she reports every word of her conversation with the innkeeper. It is only at the end of their conversation that we discover that Mr Rochester is alive.
- Making us wait until the end of the chapter to learn that Mr Rochester is living at Ferndean.
- Even at the end of the chapter, Jane has still not been reunited with Mr Rochester, thus creating more suspense for the reader.

Decision 5: Mixing Genres

By simply glancing at a text, we can immediately see that it is prose, poetry or drama. This is called the form of a text. Genre is a category of writing—for example, tragedy or comedy—and we need to read the text to learn its genre. Genre is closely linked to form, as is tells us more about what to expect in the content of the writing. Brontë employs a mixture of genres, which include:

Bildungsroman

'Bildungsroman' is a German word that translates as 'education' ('Bildung') and novel ('Roman'). A Bildungsroman is therefore a novel about the growth of a central character through several periods of life. During 'Jane Eyre', we learn of Jane's internal and external conflicts in each new geographical setting. We can track her development by how she manages these conflicts. The points in the next two paragraphs are discussed in more detail in this guide.

When we first meet Jane at Gateshead, she is an outsider because of her status as a penniless orphan and dependent on her Aunt Reed. She is unable to control her passionate temper and rebels against her cousin and aunt. She has external conflicts with her family and internal ones when she thinks she can see her uncle's 'ghost' in the red-room. Under the influence of the positive female role models of Miss Temple and Helen Burns at Lowood School, Jane learns to control her passions.

Eight years later, she is working as a governess at Thornfield Hall where she falls in love with Mr Rochester. Jane's lower social status leads her to feel unworthy of Mr Rochester; with her plain appearance, she also feels inferior to 'the beautiful Blanche'. These internal self-doubts are paralleled by the external tensions surrounding the mysteries of the laughter; Grace Poole; Mr Mason after he has been attacked; and Bertha Rochester tearing Jane's wedding veil in half. Even when she agrees to marry Mr Rochester, she feels uncomfortable with him lavishing gifts on her, resulting in more internal conflict. Still further conflict is created when she learns that he is married, and she refuses his offer to become his mistress.

In the Moor House chapters, Jane suffers internal and external conflict when she becomes a beggar. As a school mistress, she subsequently has concerns about dropping in social rank. At the end of the Moor House chapters, a huge amount of emotional and spiritual conflict is created by St. John with his marriage proposals and cold ways. Jane almost rejects her own passions and accepts his proposal, but her supernatural connection with Mr Rochester makes her realise that she must marry for love. We have emotional conflict when she learns that Rochester Hall has burnt down and she does not know if Mr Rochester is still living. Finally, we have the famous line 'Reader, I married him', which shows that Jane actively makes choices and has become, for the time being at least, the dominant partner in the relationship.

Brontë challenges the tradition of gender hierarchy by writing from the point of view of a woman. This, combined with her beliefs about how women are restricted in Victorian society, emphasises that, in her view, a woman's inner development is of equal importance to a man's.

Romance

The novel's popularity when it was published was largely due to its style of writing; as we have seen, it was unusual for a novel to be written from a first-person female perspective, especially one that describes the narrator's feelings with such intensity.

Moreover, at that time, the readership of novels was predominantly female, so Brontë's fans would better empathise with the thoughts and feelings of a female protagonist.

Jane's love interest Mr Rochester is not, like Jane, conventionally good-looking. However, with his 'dark face, stern features and heavy brow', he resembles a Byronic hero, a type of character, named after the English Romantic poet Lord Byron. A Byronic hero is a flawed hero, who is dark, mysterious, moody, rebellious, arrogant, brooding and passionate. By depicting Mr Rochester as a Byronic hero, not only Jane, but also many of her readers would be attracted to him.

Typical characteristics of the romance genre are that two people fall in love with each other, there is an obstacle, they overcome the obstacle, and they live happily ever after. In 'Jane Eyre', the obstacle is Bertha Rochester; she dies in a fire, so Jane and Mr Rochester can now marry and live happily ever after. This is a greatly simplified summary, however, which does not fully explore many important elements of the Bildungsroman genre.

The Gothic Novel

The gothic genre combines Romanticism with fiction and horror. In gothic literature, characters usually include a virtuous orphaned heroine (who faints a lot) and a murderous villain with terrifying eyes. Tales are set in the past, often in remote foreign castles or monasteries with secret subterranean passages. Expect to encounter a vampire, ghost or monster. The weather is often horrible, and there will be a lot of melodrama.

This genre was popular in the Romantic Movement but, by the 1840s, it began to decline due to an increasing appetite for more socially realistic novels (such as those of Anthony Trollope). Brontë's success was her ability to combine elements of realism with gothic melodrama. Her orphaned heroine, for example, does not faint at the sight of blood. These elements are described in detail under the *Gothic Imagery* subheading in *Theme and Context: The Spiritual and The Supernatural* section.

Settings

The novel is structured in a series of episodes based on different places. Each place or setting symbolises a new phase in Jane's life. The five main settings are as follows:

Gateshead symbolises the beginning of Jane's life. It is the gateway from which she leaves her family and heads off to her future. By the end of the Gateshead chapters, we see that the next stage in her development is to learn to control her emotions.

Lowood is called this because it is literally built in a low valley beside a wood. Symbolically, it represents low point in Jane's life. Like a person in a wood, she is confined and surrounded by circumstances that she cannot control. She learns to control her emotions but eventually becomes restless, wanting to experience the wider world.

Thornfield Hall is full of difficulties and trials, like a field of thorns. Here, Jane struggles with her jealousy for Blanche Ingram and is tempted to become Mr Rochester's mistress. There is also the mystery of the strange laugh in the middle of the night; the enigmatic Grace Poole, who apparently sets bed curtains on fire; and an increasing sense of threat from the strange woman who tears Jane's wedding veil in half. The field of thorns also has biblical connotations, creating the impression that Mr Rochester will have to reap the consequences of what he has sown.

Moor House is named after the moor upon which it was built. The vast, open space of the moor symbolises the space that Jane needs to heal. It also represents her metaphorically wandering in the desert like Jesus when he was tempted by the devil (Matthew 4:1-11). When Jane is in the wilderness of the moors, this symbolises her spiritual difficulties, her physical difficulties and her lack of direction in life. Moor House is also called Marsh End, which signifies the end of Jane's struggles through difficult times. This might be a play on words: at Marsh End, Jane ends her march.

Before Jane arrives at Moor House, the coach drops her at the *Whitcross* crossroads. This symbolises that she is at a crossroads in her life and that she needs to make decisions. Whitcross also breaks down to 'white cross', connoting that God will comfort Jane. It might also foreshadow Jane unknowingly following the path along the moors to the house of a man of God, St. John. He is associated with white imagery ('snow' – 'ice' – 'frozen sea' – 'avalanche' - 'marble'), which are the same colour as the cross, signifying that their meeting is preordained.

Ferndean suggests ferns, which grow in woods. This emphasises the isolation of the manor house, which is described with imagery of death, illness and decay. It is 'buried' in a wood and in an 'insalubrious' (run-down) state. The location is so detrimental to the health that earlier in the novel, Mr Rochester tells Jane that he would not even house Bertha there. It is therefore a place where Mr Rochester goes to die.

Ferndean might also symbolise a magical place for the couple. Just like the hidden castle in the fairy tale 'Sleeping Beauty', it is not easy to find. The entrance is concealed in the 'dense summer foliage—no opening anywhere'. Jane first sees Mr Rochester in the 'twilight', a time associated with the supernatural because it is between day and night. This suggests that the supernatural world (represented by Jane) and the human world (Mr Rochester) are coming together. The fairy tale roles are reversed with Jane rescuing Mr Rochester from his living death and despair. They now have the 'quiet island' away from others that Mr Rochester wanted (in chapter 19) where Jane can help him remove his 'hideous recollections' of the human world.

Finally, ferns suggest abundance, growth and fertility, foreshadowing Jane and Mr Rochester's marriage and children. A dean is also the head of the chapter of a cathedral, so this adds to the marriage imagery.

Setting and Contrast

Setting is used to enhance contrasts. For example, in chapter 36, Jane catches the same coach at Whitcross that she arrived in. This encourages the reader to reflect on the change in her circumstances: she is now rich and has family while before, she was 'desolate, and hopeless, and objectless'. The use of three adjectives and the repetition of 'and' slows the description for the reader and emphasises her change in fortune.

Similarly, in chapter 36 when Jane is returning to Thornfield, she sees the fields through which she had previously hurried, 'blind, deaf, distracted' when she fled Thornfield. The triplet of adverbs suggests an assault on her senses, indicating that she was mad with grief. Now, in her hurry to return to Thornfield, she states 'How fast I walked! How I ran sometimes!'. The exclamatory sentences emphasise her joy and hopes, heightening the contrast between the past and the present.

Setting and Suspense

Setting can be used to develop suspense. For example, when Jane leaves Thornfield Hall in chapter 21 to visit her dying Aunt Reed in Gateshead, this delays the development of Jane and Mr Rochester's relationship.

Structure

Because the novel is structured by setting, there is a risk of it being disjointed. Cohesion is created, however, by each section developing themes such as class, gender relations, the supernatural, etc. There are repeated motifs (reoccurring ideas), symbols and images, and the novel contains parallels and contrasts in character, theme and imagery. All of these combine through Jane's development to create a cohesive novel.

Freytag's Pyramid

Gustav Freytag was a nineteenth century German novelist who saw common patterns in the plots of stories and novels, and developed a diagram to analyse them. 'Jane Eyre' describes a series of events particular to each setting, so Freytag's pyramid will be used to analyse the events of each location. An explanation of the different parts of the pyramid is below:

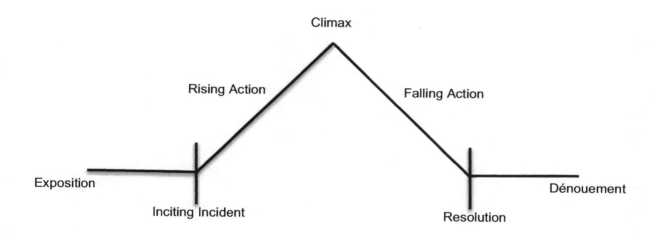

Exposition: the first part of a plot, in which the audience learns about the characters and setting.

Inciting incident: (sometimes called complication): something happens to begin the action or conflict.

Rising action: the story becomes more exciting as conflicts build.

Climax: the point of greatest tension in a play. The main character comes face-to-face with the conflict and often needs to make a choice.

Falling action: because of the climax, there are more events, but we know that the story will soon end.

Resolution: the main problem or conflict is settled.

Dénouement: the fallout in which any leftover questions, mysteries or secrets are solved.

Gateshead (Chapters 1-4)

Summaries and Structure

Chapter Summaries

Chapter 1: Ten-year-old Jane Eyre lives in Gateshead with her wealthy Aunt Reed and her cousins Eliza, Georgiana and John. John taunts Jane about being a penniless orphan and throws a book at her. When Jane loses her temper and retaliates, Mrs Reed orders her to be locked in the red-room where her uncle died.

Chapter 2: In the red-room, Jane thinks about her dead Uncle Reed, who had made her aunt promise to care for Jane as one of her own. Jane sees a moving light and thinks his ghost has returned to punish Mrs Reed for breaking her promise. Jane panics and screams, but Mrs Reed thinks that she is acting. Jane becomes hysterical and faints.

Chapter 3: Jane wakes up in her bedroom. The servants' apothecary Mr. Lloyd suggests that she is sent away to boarding school where she might be happier. Jane overhears the servants Bessie and Miss Abbot talking about her, and she learns about her parents.

Chapter 4: Two months later, Mr. Brocklehurst visits the house. Mrs Reed tells him that Jane has a tendency to lie. After he leaves, Jane vents her anger at Mrs Reed. Bessie tells Jane stories and sings songs.

Freytag's Pyramid applied to the Gateshead Chapters

Exposition: we are introduced to the characters of Jane and her family at Gateshead.

Inciting incident: John Reed throws a book at Jane and she retaliates.

Rising action: Jane is taken to the red-room where she sees a moving light, thinks that it is the ghost of her dead uncle, and becomes hysterical. The servants and Aunt Reed show no compassion.

Climax: Jane faints.

Falling action: Jane begins to recuperate. She agrees to go to school.

Resolution: Mr Brocklehurst from Lowood School visits. Jane challenges Mrs Reed (victim becomes victor).

Dénouement: Before Jane leaves Gateshead, a new mood of friendship is established with Bessie.

Lowood (Chapters 5-10)

Summaries and Structure

Chapter Summaries

Chapter 5: Jane travels alone by coach to Lowood. The following day, the kind-hearted superintendent, Miss Temple, orders lunch for the girls, as the breakfast porridge was inedible. Miss Scatcherd is cruel towards Helen Burns, whom Jane befriends.

Chapter 6: The next morning, the water in the pitchers is frozen, and the potions of food are too small. Miss Scatcherd flogs Helen for having dirty nails. Helen tells Jane that, as a Christian, it is her duty to bear punishments and to love her enemies. Jane disagrees.

Chapter 7: Three months pass. The pupils are underfed and forced to march to church without warm clothing or appropriate winter footwear. Mr Brocklehurst visits the school. He orders Jane to stand on a stool and, announcing that she is a liar (Mrs Reed had told him this), he forbids everyone to speak to her. Helen consoles Jane by smiling.

Chapter 8: At the end of the school day, Helen comforts Jane. Jane tells Miss Temple her about her life at Gateshead. Miss Temple promises to write to Mr. Lloyd to confirm Jane's story. She gives the girls tea and cake. Mr. Lloyd replies to the letter, and Miss Temple publicly declares Jane's innocence. Jane works hard at the school—she is particularly good at drawing, and her French improves.

Chapter 9: It is now spring. More than half of the pupils catch typhus, and the remaining children are left to their own devices. Jane visits Helen and learns that she is dying of consumption. The girls talk and fall asleep. During the night, Helen dies.

Chapter 10: Jane's narrative continues after a gap of eight years. She explains that the typhus epidemic drew public attention to Lowood. Following an enquiry, the school was moved to a better location, and conditions for the pupils improved. Although Mr. Brocklehurst was retained as treasurer, the school thrived under new management. Jane took advantage of her education and remained as a teacher. Miss Temple's marriage prompts the restless Jane to advertise and accept the position of governess at Thornfield Hall. Before she leaves, Bessie visits her and tells her that Mr Eyre, her father's brother, enquired after her at Gateshead.

Freytag's Pyramid applied to the Lowood School Chapters

Exposition: We are introduced to school life and its inhabitants.

Inciting incident: A combination of freezing temperatures, poor food, scant clothing and the unsanitary location of Lowood.

Rising action: Miss Scatcherd flogs Helen. Mr Brocklehurst calls Jane a liar. More than half the children catch typhus and die.

Climax: Helen Burns dies.

Falling action: The school is relocated and put under new management.

Resolution: Jane works hard, finishes her education and becomes a teacher at Lowood.

Dénouement: Miss Temple marries, so Jane applies for and is offered a position as a governess at Thornfield Hall. Bessie visits and tells Jane about her uncle.

Thornfield Hall (Chapters 11-27)

Summaries and Structure

Chapter Summaries

Chapter 11: Jane arrives at Thornfield and is welcomed by Mrs Fairfax, the housekeeper. Jane's pupil is Adèle, a young French girl whose guardian, Mr Rochester, owns the house and is frequently absent. Jane hears strange laughter, and Mrs. Fairfax tells off Grace Poole, a servant.

Translations

French	English
bonne	a nurse
C'est là ma gouverante!	This is my governess!
Mais oui, certainement.	But yes, certainly.
La Ligue des Rats: fable de La Fontaine.	The League of Rats: a fable by La Fontaine
Qu' avez vous donc? lui dit un de ces rats; parlez!	What have you got? said one of the rats; speak!
Mesdames, vous êtes servies!	Ladies, you are served!
J'ai bien faim, moi!	I'm very hungry!

Chapter 12: One afternoon, Jane volunteers to walk to nearby Hay to post a letter for Mrs Fairfax. She is sitting on a stile admiring the rising moon when a dog, a horse and rider approach. The horse slips on ice and the rider falls to the ground, so Jane helps the man. Upon her return from Hay, she recognises the dog and learns that it belongs to Mr. Rochester.

Translations

French	English
par parenthèse	by the way
Revenez bientôt, ma bonne amie, ma chère Mdlle. Jeannette	Come back soon, my good friend, my dear Miss Jane

Chapter 13: The next day, Mr. Rochester invites Jane and Adèle to have tea. He is intrigued by three of Jane's drawings. Later, Mrs. Fairfax explains that Mr Rochester did not get on well with his family and that he had inherited Thornfield upon the death of his elder brother nine years previously.

Translations

French	English
Et cela doit signifier qu'il y aura là dedans un cadeau pour moi, et peut-être pour vous aussi, mademoiselle. Monsieur a parlé de vous: il m'a demandé le nom de ma gouvernante, et si elle n'était pas une petite personne, assez mince et un peu pâle. J'ai dit qu'oui: car c'est vrai, n'est-ce pas, mademoiselle?	And this must mean that there will be a gift in there for me, and maybe for you too, miss. Monsieur has spoken of you: he asked me the name of my governess, and if she was not a small person, quite thin and pale. I said yes: because it is true, isn't it, miss?
N'est-ce pas, monsieur, qu'il y a un cadeau pour Mademoiselle Eyre dans votre petit coffre?	Is there not, sir, a gift for Miss Eyre in your little box?

Chapter 14: One evening, Mr Rochester sends for Jane and Adèle. He gives Adèle a present and asks Jane if she thinks him handsome. She says no. They talk about sin, forgiveness and redemption. Mr Rochester promises to tell Jane about Adèle's mother.

Translations

French	English
Ma boite! ma boite!	My box! My box!
…tiens-toi tranquille, enfant; comprends-tu?	…keep quiet, child; do you understand?
Oh ciel! Que c'est beau!	Oh heavens! How beautiful!
nonnette	nun
tête-à-tête	in private conversation

French	English
Il faut que je l'essaie!	I must try it on
et à l'instant même!	and at once!
Est-ce que ma robe va bien?	Does my dress look good?
et mes souliers? et mes bas? Tenez, je crois que je vais danser!	and my shoes? and my stockings? Here, I think I'm going to dance!
Monsieur, je vous remercie mille fois de votre bonté	Sir, I thank you a thousand times for your kindness.
C'est comme cela que maman faisait, n'est-ce pas, monsieur?	This is what mother did, isn't it, sir?

Chapter 15: Mr Rochester tells Jane about his affair with Adèle's mother, Céline Varens. When he discovered that she was unfaithful to him, he ended the relationship. Céline claimed that Adèle was his daughter, which he denies. She abandoned her daughter, so he made Adèle his ward and brought her to England. Later that evening, Jane hears a strange 'demoniac laugh' outside her bedroom. She smells smoke and saves Mr Rochester's life from a fire. He confirms Jane's guess that Grace Poole is responsible for the strange laughter.

Translations

French	English
grande passion	great love
taille d'athlète	athletic build
croquant	devouring
porte cochère	carriage entranceway
vicomte	viscount
beauté mâle	masculine beauty
hâuteur	arrogance

Chapter 16: The next morning, everyone believes that the fire was caused by Mr Rochester falling asleep by a lit candle. Jane learns that he has left and that he will be spending time with Blanche Ingram. Jane, who realises that she is falling in love with Mr

Rochester, tells herself off and draws an imaginary portrait of Blanche, which she compares to a portrait of her own plainer looks.

Translations

French	English
Qu' avez-vous, mademoiselle?	What's the matter, Miss?
Vos doigts tremblent comme la feuille, et vos joues sont rouges: mais, rouges comme des cerises!	Your fingers are trembling like a leaf, and your cheeks are red: but red like cherries!

Chapter 17: Jane suspects that there is more to Grace Poole than meets the eye. A week later, Mr Rochester returns with some guests, who include Blanche Ingram. Mr Rochester insists that Jane join them in the drawing room after dinner. His guests first ignore Jane, and then Blanche Ingram begins a discussion that results in the guests criticising governesses. Jane is upset and tries to leave. Mr Rochester allows her to leave but tells her that she must go to the drawing room every evening. He almost betrays his feelings for her.

Translations

French	English
Elles changent de toilettes.	They are changing their clothes.
Chez maman, quand il y avait du monde, je le suivais partout, au salon et à leurs chambres; souvent je regardais les femmes de chambre coiffer et habiller les dames, et c'était si amusant: comme cela on apprend.	At my mother's house, when we had company, I followed them everywhere, to the lounge and their bedrooms; often I watched the maids styling their hair and helping them to dress, and it was fun: that's how you learn.
Mais oui, mademoiselle: voilà cinq ou six heures que nous n'avons pas mangé.	But yes, Miss: we have not eaten for five or six hours.
et alors quel dommage!	what a pity!
Est-ce que je ne puis pas prendrie une seule de ces fleurs magnifiques, mademoiselle? Seulement pour	Can I take just one of these beautiful flowers, Miss? Just to finish off my outfit.

completer ma toilette.	
minois chiffoné	pretty face
Gardez-vous en bien!	Take care!

Chapter 18: The guests play charades. Jane believes that Mr Rochester will marry Blanche for her beauty and status and that Blanche will marry him for his money. Mr Mason, who met Mr Rochester in the West Indies, arrives at Thornfield when Mr Rochester is away from home. A gypsy woman tells the fortunes of the 'young and single' ladies. Blanche goes first but does not look happy with the results. The gypsy refuses to leave until she has spoken to Jane.

Translation

French	English
Voilà, Monsieur Rochester, qui revient!	Look! Mr Rochester's coming back!

Chapter 19: Jane realises that the gypsy is Mr Rochester in disguise. He looks shocked and troubled when she tells him that Mr Mason is in the house.

Chapter 20: Jane and the guests are woken by cries for help. Mr Rochester tells them that a servant has had a nightmare. After the guests return to their beds, Mr Rochester asks for Jane's help. On the third storey of the house, she finds Mr. Mason, who has been stabbed and bitten. She staunches his wounds. Mr Rochester forbids Mr Mason and Jane to talk to each another while he gets a surgeon, who takes Mr Mason from the house. Jane and Mr Rochester walk in the orchard, and Mr Rochester asks Jane whether a man should ignore an obstacle that has been created by society in order that he can marry. Jane says that he should look to God, not a human being, for his salvation.

Chapter 21: A servant from Gateshead brings news that, triggered by the suicide of the dissipated and debt-ridden John Reed, Mrs Reed has had a stroke and is dying. She now wants to talk to Jane. At Gateshead, Jane sees Bessie, now married with children. Her cousins Eliza and Georgiana hate each other, and Mrs Reed is still unfriendly towards Jane. Before she dies, Mrs. Reed gives Jane a three-year-old letter from John Eyre, her father's brother. He wants to adopt Jane and make her his heir; Mrs Reed had deliberately withheld the letter.

Chapter 22: Jane stays at Gateshead for a month after her aunt dies. She walks the last part of her return journey to Thornfield meets Mr Rochester, who seems happy to see her. Jane is glad to be back. Everyone at Thornfield gives her a warm welcome.

Translation

French	English
prête à croquer sa petite maman Anglaise	ready to devour her little English mother

Chapter 23: Mr Rochester pretends to tell Jane that he has decided to marry Blanche Ingram. He says that he knows of a position as a governess for Jane in Ireland. Jane is upset but, to her astonishment, he admits that he has only been talking about Blanche Ingram to make her jealous. He then he proposes to Jane under a chestnut tree. There is a storm, so they rush back to the house where Mr Rochester kisses Jane repeatedly. This is witnessed by an 'amazed' Mrs Fairfax. The next day, they learn that the chestnut tree has been split in half by a bolt of lightning.

Chapter 24: Mrs. Fairfax is suspicious of Mr Rochester's motives and advises Jane to keep him at a distance as 'Gentlemen in his station are not accustomed to marry their governesses'. To Jane's great reluctance, he insists on buying her jewellery and silk dresses. Jane insists that she will remain a governess until they marry. Uncomfortable with Mr Rochester lavishing money on her, Jane decides to write to her uncle John Eyre in Madeira to announce her pending marriage. If she inherits her uncle's fortune, she will feel more at ease with being 'kept' by Mr Rochester.

Translations

French	English
sans mademoiselle	without Miss
Oh, qu' elle y sera mal—peu comfortable!	Oh, it will be bad - uncomfortable!
un vrai menteur	a real liar
conte de fée	fairy tale
du reste, il n'y avait pas de fées, et quand même il y en avait	besides, there were no fairies, and even if there were
pour me donner une contenance	to give myself airs

Chapter 25: The night before their wedding, Jane tells Mr Rochester that the preceding evening, she awoke from bad dreams to see a 'fearful and ghastly woman', who tore

her wedding veil in half. Mr Rochester, blaming Grace Poole, suggests that Jane saw her 'in a state between sleeping and waking'. He says that he will explain why he keeps Grace in the house after they have been married for a year and a day.

Chapter 26: It is Jane's wedding day. During the ceremony, the priest asks if there are any impediments. A solicitor called Mr Briggs declares that Mr Rochester is already married. Mr Mason, also present, has signed a letter stating that fifteen years previously, Mr Rochester married his sister, Bertha, in Jamaica. Mr Rochester admits that his wife—who is mad and looked after by Grace Poole—is still alive. He insists that they visit her, and Bertha Rochester attacks him. Jane learns that Mr Mason had been in Madeira when John Eyre received her letter. Mr Eyre was on his sick bed, so he asked Mr Mason to return to England to stop the bigamous marriage.

Chapter 27: Mr Rochester proposes that he and Jane pretend to be a married couple and live in the south of France. Jane, not wanting to become his mistress, refuses. Mr Rochester explains the history of his marriage. To avoid temptation, Jane leaves Thornfield just before dawn.

Freytag's Pyramid applied to the Thornfield Hall Chapters

Exposition: Jane arrives at Thornfield, and we meet Mrs Fairfax and Adèle. There is strange laughter, which is linked to Grace Poole. The characters and setting are now established.

Inciting incident: Jane meets and helps Mr Rochester. The entire story revolves around his arrival, his impact on her and how he awakens her love and desires. He is a catalyst for the rising action.

Rising action: The fire in Mr Rochester's bedroom. Jane's jealousy of Blanche Ingram. Mr. Mason being attacked, thereby developing the mystery. Jane's visit to Gateshead and receiving John Eyre's letter. The proposal under the chestnut tree. The 'ghost', who enters Jane's bedroom and tears her bridal veil in half. Jane's nightmares prophesying doom.

Climax: Wedding day—Jane discovers that Mr Rochester is already married.

Falling action: The aftermath of events in the church. Jane sees Bertha Rochester and learns her story. Mr Rochester asks Jane to become his mistress.

Resolution: Prompted by the 'vision' of her mother who urges her to flee temptation, Jane decides to leave.

Dénouement: She leaves, 'weeping wildly'.

Moor House/Marsh End/Morton (Chapters 28-36) Summaries and Structure

Chapter Summaries

Chapter 28: Jane spends all her money on the coach fare to Whitcross and then leaves her parcel on the coach. Now 'destitute', she sleeps outside and begs in a nearby village. After another day and night, she sees a light from a house on the moor. The servant refuses to let her in, and Jane collapses. The man of the house, St. John Rivers, hears her praying and takes her inside where she is looked after. Anxious not to be discovered by Mr Rochester, she tells the Rivers siblings that her name is Jane Elliott.

Translations

German	English
Da trat hervor Einer, anzusehen wie die Sternen Nacht.	*Then one person stepped forward, looking like the stars at night.*

Commentary: this sentence could be foreshadowing Jane's arrival. Stars are celestial imagery, traditionally used by sailors to guide ships. This suggests that God has led Jane to Moor House. In chapter 33, Jane is metaphorically lit with stars: the wall 'seemed a sky thick with ascending stars,—every one lit me to a purpose or delight', which is her decision to share her inheritance with her cousins. This translation therefore foreshadows her role in the good fortune of the Rivers family.

Commentary: This is an image of someone using scales and weighing or balancing

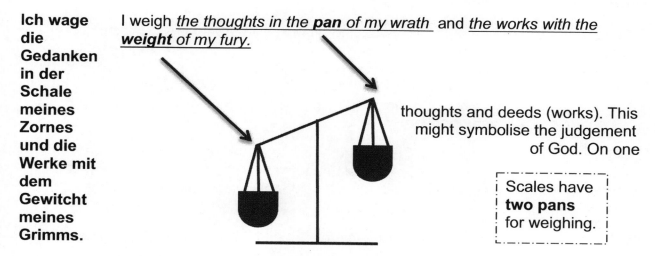

Ich wage die Gedanken in der Schale meines Zornes und die Werke mit dem Gewitcht meines Grimms.

I weigh *the thoughts in the **pan** of my wrath* and *the works with the **weight** of my fury.*

thoughts and deeds (works). This might symbolise the judgement of God. On one

Scales have **two pans** for weighing.

side, God could be angry and judging Jane who, in her thoughts, placed Mr Rochester above God ('I could not, in those days, see God for His creature: of whom I had made an idol', Chapter 24). The other side might represent God's anger with Mr Rochester's deeds when he tried to break the laws of God and humankind by attempting a bigamous marriage. Another interpretation is that Jane has been sent by God who, after weighing the situation of the Rivers family in the scales of justice (Jane later says 'justice would be done' when she decides to share her inheritance), uses Jane as his tool to restore them to their position of wealthy gentry

Chapter 29: Jane is ill for three days and nights. On the fourth day, she goes to the kitchen, and the servant Hannah apologises for turning her away. She tells Jane about St. John, a pastor, and his two sisters. Jane admits that her real name is not Jane Elliott. St. John agrees to help her to find work.

Chapter 30: Jane enjoys the company of the Rivers sisters, Diana and Mary, who are due to leave Marsh End to return to their work as governesses. St. John will resume work from the parsonage at Morton. He receives a letter with news of the death of their Uncle John, who has left all his money to another relative. Jane accepts a position as school mistress in a charity school for girls.

Chapter 31: We meet Rosamond Oliver, a wealthy heiress who finances the girls' school. Jane watches Rosamond and St. John together and concludes that they are in love. St. John tells Jane that he plans to become a missionary.

Chapter 32: St. John admits to Jane that, although he 'wildly' loves Rosamond, he is a 'cold hard man' and she would not make a good missionary's wife. He then mysteriously tears a piece off a sheet of paper and leaves the room.

Chapter 33: St. John reveals that he knows who Jane is: she had inadvertently written her signature on the previous day's scrap of paper. He explains that the solicitor Mr Briggs is looking for her, as John Eyre has died and left her twenty thousand pounds. Jane is more interested in news of Mr Rochester. She is delighted to learn that St. John, Diana and Mary are her cousins—John Eyre is also their uncle—and she decides to divide her inheritance between the four of them.

Chapter 34: Jane spends Christmas at Moor House with her cousins. Thanks to the inheritance, Diana and Mary need no longer work for a living. Rosamond becomes engaged to a rich man called Mr. Granby. St. John asks Jane to learn 'Hindustani' to help him prepare for missionary work in India. Although she agrees, she does not enjoy the process, as St. John is extremely demanding. He finally asks her to marry him. She does not love him, so she refuses.

Chapter 35: The angry St. John ('not a man to be lightly refused') spends a week pressurising Jane to marry him. She almost submits but, at that moment, she has a mystical supernatural connection with Mr Rochester and hears his voice calling her name. She replies, telling him that she is coming.

Beginning of Chapter 36: St. John leaves, and Jane bids Diana and Mary goodbye.

Freytag's Pyramid applied to the Moor House Chapters

Exposition: Jane is destitute. She sleeps rough and is reduced to begging for food. She arrives at Moor House, but the servant, Hannah, turns her away.

Inciting incident: Jane collapses, appeals to God and is taken in by St. John Rivers. She is ill for three days and nights, which gives him and his sisters, Diana and Mary, time to get to know Jane before they decide to help her.

Rising action: The Rivers' Uncle John dies and leaves his money to another relation. Jane becomes a school mistress. St. John mysteriously tears scrap off Jane's drawing paper. Jane learns that she is related to the Rivers siblings, and she inherits money from John Eyre. St. John asks her to marry him, and he refuses to take no for an answer.

Climax: Jane, moved by St. John's prayer, almost agrees to marry him. Jane asks God for guidance and, just as she is about to accept the proposal, she has a supernatural connection with Mr Rochester, who is calling her.

Falling action: Jane replies to Mr Rochester. She concludes that 'nature' has helped her, not 'witchcraft'. She rejects St. John.

Resolution: Jane decides to leave. From the start of chapter 36: St. John leaves and Jane says goodbye to Diana and Mary.

Dénouement: Jane travels by carriage to Thornfield.

Thornfield and Ferndean (Chapters 36-38) Summaries and Structure

Chapter Summaries

Remainder of chapter 36: Jane takes a coach to Thornfield, only to discover a blackened ruin. The innkeeper of the Rochester Arms tells her that several months earlier, Bertha Rochester had set Thornfield Hall on fire. Mr Rochester tried to rescue Bertha, who jumped off the battlements and died. The house collapsed around Mr Rochester, injuring him. He lives at Ferndean Manor.

Chapter 37: Jane goes to Ferndean and is reunited with Mr Rochester. She accepts his proposal of marriage. He tells her that, a few nights earlier, he had desperately cried out her name and had seemed to hear a reply.

Chapter 38: Jane and Mr Rochester marry. Mary and Diana write to congratulate her, but she hears nothing from St. John. Jane visits Adèle and moves her to a better school. Adèle grows up to be a 'pleasing and obliging companion'. The reader learns that Jane is telling her story after ten years of marriage. After two years, they have a baby boy. At the same time, Mr Rochester begins to regain the sight in his remaining eye. Diana and Mary both marry, St. John goes to India, but has a premonition that he will die.

Freytag's Pyramid applied to the Thornfield/ Ferndean Chapters

Exposition: Jane arrives and decides to walk the final two miles.

Inciting incident: She discovers the 'blackened ruin' of Thornfield Hall.

Rising action: She questions the innkeeper and learns about the fates of Bertha and Mr Rochester. Jane goes to Ferndean.

Climax: They are reunited.

Falling action: Mr Rochester learns about what Jane has been doing since she last saw him. She teases him about St. John, making him jealous.

Resolution: Mr Rochester proposes and Jane accepts.

Dénouement: They marry. Mr Rochester regains some of his sight. They have a son. We learn about what has happened to the Rivers siblings and Adèle.

Language

Symbolism of Literature, Music and Art

Literature

Brontë deliberately uses symbolism (where something represents something else) when referring to literature within the novel. For example, at Gateshead, the young Jane is reading Bewick's 'History of Birds', and the reference to 'birds' in the title symbolises or represents Jane's wish to leave the nest and escape the tyrannies of her family. This is supported by Brontë's use of pathetic fallacy (where the weather or environment reflect a character's feelings): like the 'sea-fowl' that live in remote 'Norway' on 'solitary rocks', Jane feels isolated and lonely. Norway is a cold country in the north and Brontë lists additional countries in the 'vast sweep of the Arctic Zone' to build her feelings of desolation and unhappiness.

In the extract from Bewick, there are many images of coldness and death: 'frost and snow', 'firm fields of ice, the accumulation of centuries of winters' and 'extreme cold'. This semantic field (thematically linked vocabulary) emphasises Jane's position as an orphan, as it is a metaphor for how she is frozen out of the Reed family. However, the references to other countries in the extract introduce the idea of life beyond Gateshead, anticipating her departure for Lowood at the end of the Gateshead chapters.

The pictures in Bewick's book also have a positive effect on Jane because they stimulate her imagination: she uses 'each picture' to create 'a story' that is 'profoundly interesting'. This serves as a coping mechanism for the harsh, cold realities of her life at Gateshead. It also stimulates a love of learning that promises well for her future progress at Lowood and subsequent career as a governess and teacher.

After the red-room incident, Bessie gives the recuperating Jane 'Gulliver's Travels' to read. Written by Jonathan Swift, this is the story of Gulliver, who travels to faraway lands where he is treated as an outsider. The story mirrors Jane's feelings of being an outsider at Gateshead and foreshadows her future travels to Lowood, Thornfield, Moor House and Ferndean. Jane, like Gulliver, will be an outsider in the future as well as the present. At Thornfield, for example, she will be called 'a fairy', an 'elf' and other words from the supernatural world, which emphasise her difference.

Bessie reads to the children from 'Pamela'. 'Pamela, or Virtue Rewarded' by Samuel Richardson, is about a young servant girl whose master tries to seduce her; it was considered a rather daring novel in its time. Pamela resists every attempt at seduction until finally her master proposes marriage. This obviously has parallels with the Thornfield chapters with Mr Rochester being an older man, who tries to make Jane his mistress. Some of the events in 'Pamela' therefore foreshadow those in 'Jane Eyre'. Perhaps Jane had the novel in the back of her mind when she first met Mr Rochester at Thornfield.

Bessie also reads to the children from 'Henry, Earl of Moreland' a novel by Henry Brook. The novel's hero (or protagonist) often fights against repression, like Jane. Perhaps

Bronte invites us to think of him as a role model for Jane in her struggles against the odds. Bronte might also be suggesting that there will be many obstacles in Jane's life that she will need to overcome.

When Jane first meets Helen at Lowood School, Helen is reading 'Rasselas', an essay by Samuel Johnson, which argues that life is to be endured rather than enjoyed (happiness is often unobtainable). Brontë might be associating Helen with the essay because she is being persecuted by the bullying Miss Scatcherd. Brontë might additionally be hinting at the problems with Helen's health that will result in her death. Finally, the author might be suggesting that 'Rasselas' is a source of comfort for Helen: although she will never live to experience earthly happiness, she can hope for spiritual happiness in the afterlife.

Music

In the novel, music has symbolic meaning for Jane, as it reflects her emotions. For example, Bessie sings a ballad that tells the story of a 'poor orphan child' wandering through wild 'mountains', 'moors' and 'rocks'. The child's only consolation is that God will save her ('God is a friend to the poor orphan child'). The underlying message is that Jane should look to 'heaven' to comfort her. The ballad foreshadows Jane's future when she wanders in the wilderness of the moors before arriving at Moor House; St. John, whom she will meet, is associated with the hardness of rocks. In the song, Jane (symbolised as the child) bursts into tears, as the message of the lyric provides her with the poor consolation of God as her 'comfort and hope'. This contrasts with Jane the adult later in the novel, who will find comfort in God, especially when she appeals to Him and is answered with a psychic or mystical connection with Mr Rochester. The ballad therefore reflects her current feelings and indicates her future.

Art

The three drawings that Jane shows Mr Rochester in chapter 13 also link to the theme of the supernatural. She tells the reader that she imagined them with a 'spiritual eye' before creating them. Mr Rochester states that 'the thoughts, they are elfish'. The shared use of other-worldly language suggests a spiritual connection between the couple. Fate is also implied: if Jane saw the subject matter with a 'spiritual eye', perhaps the same 'kind fairy' at Lowood that prompted her to advertise and come to Thornfield was involved. The drawings might therefore have the desired result of attracting the attention of Mr Rochester; it is almost as if the couple are characters in a fairy story, being directed by higher powers.

The unusual choice of the subject matter of the paintings reveals Jane's imagination. In addition, they foreshadow elements of Mr Rochester's description of being in love with Céline Varens. For example, in Jane's first drawing there is 'a drowned corpse' floating and the 'foam' of turbulent water. In her third drawing, there is 'a colossal head, inclined towards the iceberg, and resting against it'. Both these images convey powerlessness and being at the mercy of a current. The water reflects Mr Rochester's description of being in love: 'Floating on with closed eyes and muffled ears, you neither see the rocks bristling not far off in the bed of the flood, nor hear the breakers boil at their base.'

Again, there is the idea of being powerless, unable to control the environment, and a sense of danger lurking in the background. There is a difference between Jane and Mr Rochester's use of imagery, however. With Jane, the 'corpse' and death imagery of the 'ice-berg' with its possible decapitated head might reflect that her senses or passions have not fully awakened. Mr Rochester, on the other hand, is totally aware of what is happening and he chooses to have 'closed eyes' and 'muffled ears', indicating his willingness to allow his passions to control him. Nevertheless, Mr Rochester might be emotionally connecting with Jane through her pictures and glimpsing her supressed passionate nature.

Jane's pictures foreshadow Mr Rochester's revelations about his uncontrollable passionate love for Céline Varens. In Jane's third drawing, we have the contrasts of hopelessness ('glassiness of despair') and, in the second drawing, beauty and hope where 'rising into the sky' is a 'vision of the Evening Star'. This is like the contrasting emotions in Mr Rochester's description of love when he says: 'either you will be dashed to atoms on crag points, or lifted up and borne on by some master-wave into a calmer current—as I am now.' The 'calmer current' symbolises Jane. This develops the spiritual connection between the two and the subconscious hope from Mr Rochester that she will soothe and heal him.

Another form of art—portraiture—is used within the novel to convey themes. When Jane draws a self-portrait entitled 'Portrait of a Governess, disconnected, poor, and plain', it is interesting to examine the order of adjectives. First is status, then money, then looks, reflecting how Jane feels about her position in society. The second portrait emphasises the different physical qualities of 'Blanche, an accomplished lady of rank'. We are reminded that being 'accomplished' was a means to attract a husband, hinting at Jane's concerns about her rival, while 'lady of rank' vividly emphasises the difference between Blanche and Jane, making Blanche a better match in the eyes of society for Mr Rochester. The use of adjectives therefore highlights the differences between the two women who serve as foils to each other; however, by emphasising the differences between herself and Blanche, Jane fails to consider that on a spiritual level she is Mr Rochester's equal and might be Blanche's superior.

Finally, Brontë uses portraiture to emphasise the theme of passion versus restraint. Knowing that St. John is in love with Rosamond, Jane offers to make him a copy of the portrait of Rosamond that she is drawing. St. John says 'She is well named the Rose of the World, indeed!'. She is symbolised as a beautiful flower of the earth. When he refuses the portrait, he says 'cui bono?' which is Latin for 'to whose profit?'. In other words, what would be the point in having a copy of the portrait when he will never marry the original. He rationalises his love for Rosamond and, by mastering his passions, he symbolically rejects a flower of the earth in favour of his work for God.

The above are just some examples of how literature, music and art have symbolic meaning in Jane Eyre. As you re-read the novel, look for more and conduct some research of your own!

Pathetic Fallacy

Pathetic fallacy is when the thoughts and feelings of characters are reflected in the description of their natural or inanimate environments. For example, after Mr Brocklehurst publicly names Jane a liar, her name is cleared, and her happier thoughts are revealed in the world of her imagination with her make-believe drawings of:

> *freely pencilled houses and trees, picturesque rocks and ruins, *Cuyp-like groups of cattle, sweet paintings of butterflies hovering over unblown roses, of birds picking at ripe cherries, of wren's nests enclosing pearl-like eggs, wreathed about with young ivy sprays.*

> ***Cuyp**: *a Dutch landscape artist*

The pathetic fallacy signifies a change in mood, as Jane's tone becomes more positive. Her adjectives ('freely', 'picturesque', 'sweet', 'unblown', 'ripe' 'pearl-like' and 'young') have positive connotations, illustrating her new attitude to being a pupil at Lowood. The nature imagery also reflects this stage of her life: the 'pearl-like eggs' are as yet unhatched, reminding the reader that Jane is still a young girl, full of potential. Likewise, the 'ivy sprays' are 'young', which might represent Jane who, like ivy, is growing and searching to establish a place for herself in the world. Structurally, this passage heralds the advance of spring, which is described in the next chapter.

The opening paragraphs of the next chapter (chapter 9) begin with more pathetic fallacy. We see the lessening of Jane's 'deprivations', and she embraces the joys of spring. We understand her state of mind through her use of nature imagery. Flowers are personified (they 'peeped out amongst the leaves'), creating a playful, childlike tone, reflecting Jane's happy outdoor games. The beautiful natural world, like Jane, is bursting with new life and energy with its 'snow-drops, crocuses' and so on. These are the first flowers of the year, reflecting Jane's youth. Structurally, this section sets the reader up to be shocked when we next learn that half the pupils have caught typhus. The fertile spring imagery of new beginnings contrasts with the death imagery of the personified 'pestilence' that 'breathed typhus through its crowded schoolroom and dormitory', heightening the contrast between life and death.

There is more pathetic fallacy when Jane walks with Mr Rochester in his garden in chapter 20. Nature is now bursting with life in a mature garden, reflecting that Jane is a young woman. Mr Rochester's garden contains 'apple trees, pear trees, and cherry trees on one side, and a border on the other full of all sorts of old-fashioned flowers'. The established trees and 'old-fashioned flowers' remind the reader that Mr Rochester is older than Jane. Jane states 'The stocks, sweet-williams, primroses, pansies, mingled with southernwood, sweet-briar, and various fragrant herbs'. The verb 'mingled' reflects the couple's walk with its connotations of a courting couple. Interestingly, 'southernwood' was believed to have the properties of an aphrodisiac. At one time, young men would include it in a bouquet, so it is also known as lad's love and maid's ruin, foreshadowing Mr Rochester's later proposal that Jane become his mistress. The 'stocks' and seductive 'fragrant herbs' create a heady mixture of romance. In what appears to be a romantic gesture, Mr Rochester says 'Jane, will you have a flower?'

and she accepts the 'half-blown' rose, which could symbolise her timidity: she is like a half-opened flower, yet to fully open and blossom. Interestingly, we associate roses with England—Jane is an English rose. Mr Rochester's choice of flower to offer Jane therefore implies his rejection of Bertha.

In chapter 23, just before the proposal of marriage, Mr Rochester and Jane walk in the garden again. This time, the garden is full of fertility imagery: the gooseberry tree is 'laden' with fruit as 'large as plums' and Mr Rochester eats a 'ripe cherry'. There is also spiritual pleasure with the 'incense' of the 'sweet-briar and southernwood, jasmine, pink, and rose' and the sound of the 'nightingale warbling'. The use of pathetic fallacy and sensory language depicts the couple at the pinnacle of their relationship.

After Jane accepts Mr Rochester's proposal, the pathetic fallacy with the storm symbolises that Mr Rochester's 'dark prime' is over. The personification of the 'writhing and groaning' chestnut tree suggests God's disapproval of the proposed bigamous marriage and foreshadows the tragedy that is to come. The next day, Jane learns that the chestnut tree was struck by lightning in the night and 'half of it split away', signifying Jane's departure. The tree might also symbolise Mr Rochester's disabilities after the fire, as what remains might 'form one tree—a ruin, but an entire ruin'. There is an element of hope to their relationship, however: Jane sees that there is a 'firm base and strong roots', suggesting that their relationship will flourish.

After the failed wedding in chapter 26, ice imagery is used as pathetic fallacy to signal the death of Jane's expectations. She refers to herself as 'an ardent, expectant woman—almost a bride' becoming once again a 'cold, solitary girl', thus reminding the reader of her childhood in Gateshead when she was reading Bewick's 'History of British Birds'. We have similar winter imagery but this time it contrasts with imagery of ripeness and abundance to make clear the crushing of her hopes: 'A Christmas frost had come at midsummer; a white December storm had whirled over June; ice glazed the ripe apples'. Everything that she describes is a physical impossibility (for example, a 'A Christmas frost' cannot 'come at midsummer'), reflecting her shock as she struggles to come to terms with what has happened.

Another example of pathetic fallacy is in chapter 30 when Jane and the Rivers sisters are fascinated by the surrounding moors. The sisters 'clung' to the moors 'with a perfect enthusiasm of attachment', illustrating a desire to stay at home and a reluctance to resume their positions as governesses. Jane understands 'the fascination of the locality. I felt the consecration of its loneliness'. The noun 'consecration' means association with the sacred, so the landscape plays an important spiritual and almost religious role, comforting Jane in her loneliness. The fact that Jane and the Rivers sisters share the same feelings about the moors shows their rank of equals—all three are governesses. In addition, Jane's spiritual and emotional agreement with them reveals their kindred spirit and prepares the reader for the revelation that they are related.

In the same chapter, the wilderness of the moor conveys Jane's turbulent emotions. The use of antonyms (opposites) with lists ('strong blast and the soft breeze; the rough and the halcyon day; the hours of sunrise and sunset; the moonlight and the clouded night') illustrates her fluctuating emotions, which are part of her healing process.

At the start of chapter 37, there is pathetic fallacy with Ferndean described by Jane as 'a desolate spot', reflecting Mr Rochester's isolation and sadness. This is emphasised through the 'sad sky, cold gale, and continued small penetrating rain', which creates the impression that his unhappiness is never-ending. As we saw in the *Settings* chapter, there is a lot of death imagery with the 'dank and green' – 'decaying walls', suggesting Mr Rochester's deterioration because of his physical disabilities and depression. The 'dim light' symbolises his blindness (but being 'dim', it provides hope that his eyesight will start to return). Mr Rochester feels 'desolate and abandoned—my life dark, lonely, hopeless'. The pathetic fallacy therefore suggests that he has gone to Ferndean to die.

The above are just some examples of pathetic fallacy—there are many more! Pathetic fallacy is such a dominant literary device that it is worth memorising a few examples so that you can include them (always remembering to keep them relevant!) in exam answers.

The Colour Red

The colour 'red' is a motif (a recurring image) in the novel. When we first meet Jane, she has hidden herself behind the 'red' curtains on the window seat and is reading Bewick's 'History of Birds'. Cocooning herself in the curtains creates comforting womb imagery. It also suggests that, like an unborn baby, she has not yet entered the world, which reminds us of the symbolism of the word Gateshead.

This womb imagery contrasts with the horror of the 'red-room' at the end of the chapter when Jane is isolated and surrounded by the colour 'red'. The symbolism becomes hellish, and she faints because of the overwhelming horror of seeing the ghostly light. Whenever Jane suffers in the future, she will reference the red-room. In chapter 8, for example, when Jane is treated badly at Lowood (emotionally imprisoned), she tells Miss Temple about the 'frightful episode' in the red-room. In chapter 27, before she leaves Mr Rochester, she dreams of being a child in the red-room and the ghost of her mother urging her to 'flee temptation' to avoid being imprisoned by her passions. Consequently, the red-room symbolises spiritual, intellectual and emotional imprisonment, past, present and future.

The symbolism of the colour red changes, depending on Jane's state of mind. In chapter 3, for example, the red motif continues with her nightmare of 'a terrible red glare with thick black bars'. The 'terrible red glare' connotes being stared at in anger and has associations with the supernatural while the 'thick black bars' suggest the impossibility of escaping from a prison. This symbolises Jane's imprisonment in the red-room and could also represent her life at Gateshead which, at this point in the chapter, she has no hope of leaving. The fire imagery then changes into a reassuring 'nursery fire', which links with Mr Lloyd and Jane's positive feelings of 'inexpressible relief, a soothing conviction of protection and security'.

As Jane grows up, the colour red becomes associated with passion (see *Theme and Context: Passion versus Restraint*).

The colour red is also used as pathetic fallacy to structure tension in the novel. In chapter 25, the night before the wedding, the moon is:

> blood-red and half overcast; she seemed to throw on me one bewildered, dreary glance, and buried herself again instantly in the deep drift of cloud. The wind fell, for a second, round Thornfield; but far away over wood and water, poured a wild, melancholy wail: it was sad to listen to.

This description of the personified 'blood-red and half-overcast' moon and 'melancholy' wind suggests secrets and sadness. The moon might also symbolise the mad Bertha Rochester, or it could herald unfulfilled passions between Jane and Mr Rochester: the incompleteness of the moon reminds the reader of the torn wedding veil that is 'in two parts', foreshadowing the separation of Jane and Mr Rochester. This imagery contrasts with the end of the chapter when the 'moon shone peacefully' and Jane says 'the night is serene, sir; and so am I'. As we already know, appearances are deceptive. This is the lull before the metaphorical storm in the next chapter, which heightens the shock of the wedding day revelations.

Other Symbolism

Porridge

Porridge symbolises the lowest level of deprivation, humiliation and hopelessness possible. At Lowood, the pupils are served 'burnt porridge', which is described as so inedible that 'famine itself soon sickens over it'. The personification of 'famine' emphasises how disgusting the food is. When Jane becomes a beggar, she eats a 'stiffened mould' of porridge that is destined for a pig. She is grateful and devours it 'ravenously', contrasting with her rejection of the burnt porridge as a child. This reflects the depths to which she has been reduced.

Theme and Context: Social Class

Social class, attitudes towards class and Jane's position in the social hierarchy are recurring themes within the novel. A simplified form of the social structure of the time is as follows:

Upper Classes

The upper classes did not work. Their income was from inheritances (usually in the form of property which generated rents) or investments. There were three tiers:

- Top: royalty
- Middle-upper: other titles
- Lower-upper: wealthy country gentlemen like Mr Rochester and large-scale businessmen, bankers, etc.

Middle Classes

The middle classes worked, but as smaller-scale businessmen, lawyers, doctors, school masters, clergy, etc. They were often paid a salary monthly or annually. There were two tiers:

- Upper-middle: high salaries and social status
- Lower-middle: employed by the upper-middle class

Working Classes

This class got its hands dirty with manual work. They were often paid wages by the day or week. There were two tiers:

- Top: skilled labourers
- Bottom: unskilled labourers

The Underclass

This comprised:

- The extreme poor, who depended on charity e.g. from the workhouse or begging. This category includes the homeless and orphans. The adult underclass might be unemployed because of chronic illness, disability, age or being a single parent.
- Habitual criminals
- Prostitutes

Punctuation note: use a hyphen when creating an adjective (e.g. Mr Rochester is an upper-class person). Do not use a hyphen with the noun (e.g. Mr Rochester is a member of the upper class).

Class Conflict

Jane's Class

The Gateshead chapters introduce us to the theme of Jane as an outsider in a class-ridden society: she is a dependent in the house and therefore vulnerable. Miss Abbot tells Jane that she is 'less than a servant' because she does no work to support herself, and Bessie reminds Jane that she is 'under obligations to Mrs Reed: she keeps you: if she were to turn you off, you would have to go to the Poorhouse' (commonly known as the workhouse). The working-class servants feel that they are superior to Jane, suggesting that they regard her as one of the underclass. To them, she is a penniless orphan, and this defines her status. Jane's social status is, however, not quite so easy to define. She cannot claim the same social status as her rich family yet, being waited on in the house, she is above a servant, despite what they themselves say.

Moreover, Jane's social status is continually redefining itself. At Gateshead, she learns that her father was a 'poor clergyman'. In the Victorian times, clergymen held respected positions in society, so this information contradicts Mrs Reed's comment about Jane coming from a 'beggarly set'. There is a huge difference between a 'poor' but respected middle-class clergyman and a 'beggarly set', which suggests the underclass. Jane therefore has more respectable parentage than she was first led to believe.

Jane's social status continues to redefine itself when Bessie visits her at Lowood. Part of Bessie's function is to help the reader to evaluate Jane's accomplishments and position in society. She tells Jane that her uncle, John Eyre, 'looked quite a gentleman' when he visited Gateshead, which leads the servant to believe that the Eyres 'are as much gentry as the Reeds are'. The reference to John Eyre looking like a gentleman would elevate Jane's class status in the eyes of contemporary readers; a modern reader might be more likely to judge Jane as a 'lady' because of her accomplishments rather than her family's position. Nevertheless, the reference to John Eyre makes it easier to believe her future elevation of class when she inherits his money.

Jane's hard-to-define position within society's class structure is continued with Mr Rochester's reaction upon meeting her for the first time in chapter 12. He notes that she is 'not a servant' and he seems 'puzzled' about her position at Thornfield Hall. Like many of his contemporaries, he categorises people according to their place in the social hierarchy. Jane does not initially appear to fit within the social hierarchy, and this makes her intriguing to him.

Even when Jane's status plummets at the beginning of the Moor House chapters, her position in the class hierarchy is still blurred because 'an ordinary beggar is frequently an object of suspicion; a well-dressed beggar inevitably so'. At first sight, she is therefore neither a conventional beggar nor a rich lady; this reveals the importance of social class and looking the part. Furthermore, her appearance is misinterpreted, as we see when the servant Hannah turns Jane away from Moor House, saying: 'You are not what you ought to be, or you wouldn't make such a noise'. This comment implies that Jane is not behaving as a vagrant should. Perhaps Brontë wants to convey a moral message to the Victorian public about the importance of helping the poor, regardless of their appearance. As the daughter of a clergyman, she would have been keenly aware of the morality of behaving charitably.

Upper-Class Abuse of Power

We see a lot of examples of the upper classes abusing their power in the novel. The young Jane challenges John Reed's behaviour when she calls him a 'murderer', 'slave-driver' and 'Roman emperor'. Her use of hyperbole (exaggeration) illustrates how she struggles to control her feelings about how she has been treated: she has a strong sense of justice and will defend herself if she feels that she has been wronged, regardless of who the other person is and the consequences of her behaviour. This emphasises her immaturity at this stage of the novel. Her choice of vocabulary reveals the breadth of her learning and interest in the wider world, foreshadowing her future progress at Lowood School. The argument also foreshadows future conflicts (internal as well as external) that are class-related; for example, Jane's emotional turmoil when she believes that Mr Rochester will marry upper-class Blanche Ingram.

Brontë uses contrast to show that wealth and status are not always an indication of good character. For example, when Bessie visits Jane at Lowood (chapter 10), she says that Jane looks 'like a lady' and is 'charmed' when Jane plays the piano, draws and speaks French better than her cousins Georgiana and Eliza Reed. John Reed, we learn, is now 'a dissipated young man'. Jane looks and behaves more like a member of the upper class than her cousins, so it is ironic that their social status is higher. Through the contrast between Jane and her Reed cousins, Brontë encourages the reader to judge people by the example they set rather than by the class into which they are born.

As a young woman, Jane herself is keenly aware that wealth and status are not always a good indication of character. She quizzes Mrs Fairfax about Mr Rochester and learns that 'Mr. Rochester was Mr. Rochester in her eyes; a gentleman, a landed proprietor—nothing more'. Jane is frustrated to receive such limited information, as Mrs Fairfax can only see as far as his social status. Jane wants to learn about his character, knowing from the Reed household and Mr Brocklehurst that status does not always equate to a good character.

This point is developed in the novel when we learn some upper-class attitudes towards governesses in wealthy households. For example, in chapter 17, Jane is excluded socially from Mr Rochester's guests because of social hierarchies and her gender, contributing to her feeling of isolation. Foremost among these guests is Blanche Ingram, whom Jane describes as 'the very type of majesty'. The use of 'majesty' suggests that, at Thornfield, Jane believes her to be at the top of the social hierarchy, but Blanche's name, which means *white*, is ironic. The colour white connotes goodness, but she does not present a good example of how a member of the upper class should behave. Despite knowing that Jane can hear her, she calls governesses 'detestable' and 'ridiculous'. Perhaps Blanche is so aggressive because she suspects that Jane is a potential rival for Mr Rochester's affections. Nevertheless, these adjectives reveal a supercilious attitude and, by sneering at governesses in front of a governess, Brontë encourages the reader to judge the upper classes in general. This contrasts with Mrs Fairfax, who accepts them at face value.

The reader also learns that governesses in upper-class houses were not encouraged to marry their social equals. Blanche's mother says 'there are a thousand reasons why liaisons between governesses and tutors should never be tolerated'. She does not itemise what the 'thousand reasons' are, so the reader assumes that they are based on prejudice. Jane comments that Lady Ingram's 'fierce and hard eye' is like Mrs. Reed's; their psychological bullying of Jane is very similar, as they both lack empathy and make her painfully aware of her place in the social hierarchy.

Etiquette dictated that members of the upper classes spoke to new people only after they had been introduced. When Jane is invited to the drawing room at Thornfield Hall after dinner, Blanche and the other guests mostly ignore Jane. Not only is this because formal introductions have not taken place but, as a governess, she is of a lower social status to them and is therefore not worthy of notice. Jane has the appearance, manners and education of a lady, but these are not valued by the guests who, it seems to us, are openly ill-mannered.

Respectable Behaviour

The Rivers family demonstrate different values to the upper classes when they judge Jane. When she is ill, Jane reports the siblings' conversations about her, which focus on her education: she is 'not an uneducated person' and 'her accent was quite pure'. They also note Jane's respectability; her clothes are 'little worn and fine', and her face does not show 'vulgarity or degradation'. This contrasts with the upper classes where status, money and connections are valued more highly.

The Rivers sisters, with their intelligence and behaviour, serve as foils to the Reed sisters. They also serve as a foil to Blanche Ingram, who is egocentric. We learn that the Rivers are old established 'gentry' fallen on hard times, and the sisters treat Jane with compassion and consideration. Diana has 'charm' and Mary is 'equally intelligent' so, despite their poverty, they provide an example in the novel of what was considered proper behaviour. This is a direct contrast to the Reed sisters and Blanche Ingram. Through the Rivers sisters, Brontë therefore criticises the behaviour of the upper classes.

In chapter 30, we see that Jane and the Rivers sisters are like-minded friends of the same social class: they have an education, no parents and are governesses. As such, their education and shared intellectual bond is to their mutual advantage. Jane borrows books, which they discuss in the evenings: 'Thought fitted thought; opinion met opinion'. The repetition of 'thought' and 'opinion' emphasises the harmony of agreement on both sides. There is also an equal exchange of skills when Jane teaches Mary how to draw and Diana teaches German to Jane. Brontë went to Brussels in 1842 to polish her French, as the ability to speak another language qualified governesses and teachers to earn a higher wage. We therefore see that, despite the pleasure that Jane and the sisters derive from education, there is a distinct financial advantage to developing their knowledge and skills.

Prejudice and the Working Classes

In the novel, we see how easily young children can be influenced by class prejudice when the apothecary Mr Lloyd asks Jane is she would like to live with her poor relations. She declines because she does not understand that people can be poor and respectable: 'poverty for me was synonymous with degradation'. The young Jane appears to have absorbed the prejudices of the Reeds. She does not want to live with her relations 'at the price of caste' (in other words, she does not want to move down in class). Even though she is subject to bullying behaviour at Gateshead, Jane does not yet fully understand that the upper classes can degrade themselves.

Inverted class prejudice is implied in chapter 11 when the man who meets Jane is late at the George Inn. He does not apologise and he speaks 'abruptly', making the reader wonder if, in a society where everyone is expected to know their place, he resents her higher status. Brontë emphasises the class differences between the two by not giving the man a name, suggesting that as a member of the working classes his identity is unimportant. Moreover, spelling is used to show his regional dialect, lack of education, and to emphasise the difference in social class: 'You're noan so far fro' Thornfield now'. This episode with the man introduces the theme of class to the chapter, which is developed when Jane arrives at Thornfield Hall.

It is interesting that Jane herself shows class prejudice against Hannah, the Rivers' servant, at Moor House. When Jane first goes downstairs, she joins Hannah in the kitchen. Jane explains to the reader that it is 'well known' that 'prejudices…are most difficult to eradicate from the heart whose soil has never been loosened or fertilised by education'. The farming imagery creates the idea that education liberates, fertilises and enriches the mind, encouraging spiritual growth. Jane berates Hannah for her earlier prejudice towards her ('you ought not to consider poverty a crime') and Hannah apologises. We now see irony because Hannah's apology clearly contradicts Jane's point about the uneducated being unable to rethink their prejudices. Perhaps Brontë includes this conversation to encourage the reader to reflect on their attitudes towards the working classes.

Maintaining Class Boundaries

At Thornfield Hall, Jane is warmly welcomed by Mrs Fairfax who, being of higher status than the servants but of lower status than Mr Rochester, is keenly aware of class divisions. Despite liking John and his wife Leah, Mrs Fairfax keeps her distance because 'they are only servants, and one can't converse with them on terms of equality; one must keep them at due distance for fear of losing one's authority'. She speaks about them quite dismissively ('only servants') and the use of the formal 'one' and alliteration with 'due distance' emphasises their differences in class and education. Her formal and polished speech also contrasts with the man's dialect and abruptness earlier in the chapter (we now learn that his name is John), further developing the theme of class.

Through Mrs Fairfax, the reader learns the price of maintaining rigid class boundaries. She describes how for four winter months, she was 'quite melancholy with sitting night after night alone'. The contemporary reader might feel sorry for her, as the repetition of 'night' followed by the long vowel sound in 'alone' slows time down and emphasises her isolation. Alternatively, a modern reader might be less sympathetic because the situation is of her own making. This is an example of how the interpretation of a novel can change over time. Jane, who is higher than a servant but lower than the master, is of a similar status to Mrs Fairfax, who greets her as an equal: 'now you are here I shall be quite gay'. (In this context, 'gay' means happy.) Mrs Fairfax's warm welcome is important because it signifies the start of Jane feeling that Thornfield Hall is a home.

Class and Internal Conflict

The theme of class in the early Thornfield Hall chapters inflames Jane's internal tension and conflict. Spiritually, Jane and Mr Rochester relate to each other as equals but Jane, as a governess, is a paid employee and is therefore unsuitable to become Mr Rochester's wife. As we have seen, Brontë herself worked for short periods of time as a governess in the late 1830s. Like Jane, she was aware of the class differences between a governess and an employer. This point is emphasised in chapter 16 when Jane speculates about the 'the probability of a union between Mr. Rochester and the beautiful Blanche'. The alliteration of 'beautiful Blanche' emphasises not only the difference in status but also the difference in appearance between the two women in a time when women were judged by their looks.

As we have already seen with Bessie's comments, the reader is aware that Jane is better educated than her Reed cousins and has the manners of an aristocrat; however, her intelligence, education and refinement further confuse her ambiguous social place in the Thornfield household and worsen her internal tensions.

Mr Rochester makes Jane's internal conflict worse when he addresses her as his spiritual equal. For example, he says 'You are my little friend, are you not?' and Jane decorously replies 'I like to serve you, sir, and to obey you in all that is right.' He, perhaps deliberately, forgets that Jane is subservient to him. He might be making a literal reference to Jane's small stature; alternatively, he might be using the adjective 'little' in a patronising way. It is therefore interesting to see that Jane reminds him of his place, often addressing him as 'sir' or 'master', so she makes a conscious effort to maintain class boundaries. She also reminds him of her place with the verbs 'serve' and 'obey', revealing her conviction that, because of the class differences, there can be no hope of marriage between them.

Breaking Class Boundaries

As well as forgetting Jane's status, Mr Rochester deliberately breaks class boundaries when he discards his identity of an upper-class gentleman and disguises himself as lower-class gypsy woman. This makes the class differences in their relationship still more ambiguous and foreshadows how he will later break class boundaries when he attempts to marry Jane.

Nevertheless, we come to understand that the couple's love transcends class divisions. In chapter 23, Jane's love cannot be confined by class as she 'naturally and inevitably' loves Mr Rochester. The adverbs support the idea that Jane and Mr Rochester are fated to be together in a course of events beyond their control. This is supported by Mr Rochester's use of supernatural imagery: he feels that he has 'a string…tightly and inextricably knotted to a similar string' on Jane, suggesting that, not only are they metaphorically tied together, but they are connected by magic. After Jane accuses him of treating her like 'a machine without feelings', she demands equality and respect: 'my spirit that addresses your spirit; just as if both had passed through the grave, and we stood at God's feet, equal,—as we are!'. Jane appeals to religion to show that they are spiritual equals in the eyes of God. We therefore have a combination of destiny, the supernatural and religion to emphasise the strength of their mutual love. This suggests that their love is sufficiently powerful to transcend the class divisions, which appear now to be trivial in comparison.

After Jane accepts his proposal, Mr Rochester tries to elevate her to his social position by sending for the family jewels: 'every privilege, every attention shall be yours that I would accord a peer's daughter, if about to marry her'. At this point, Jane resists change. She objects to new clothes, as she would feel 'a jay in borrowed plumes'. A jay is a predominantly brown bird, which fits Jane's preference for wearing darker colours. The metaphor of wearing 'borrowed plumes' (or feathers) emphasises her discomfort: Jane feels that she would be 'tricked out in stage-trappings'. The stage imagery reflects brightly coloured costumes, and it implies that she is there for others to admire. The verb 'tricked out' suggests that she is being decorated, and we can almost feel Jane's contempt. The proposed elevation of her class creates an identity issue for Jane: she does not this want to be turned into something she is not. She wants to be herself. This theme is developed in the *Gender Roles and Relations* section of this guide.

Theme and Context: Gender Roles and Relations

Respectability

With the middle and upper classes, respectability and a good reputation were extremely important. As a single Victorian woman, Jane has no family to make enquiries on her behalf about the propriety of working as a governess at Thornfield Hall. This is an essential plot device for chapter 10: had enquiries been made, it is likely that she would not have accepted a position looking after an illegitimate child, who is reputed to be the daughter of a supposedly single man with a history of mistresses.

Jane believes that her reputation will be secure when she receives the letter from Mrs Fairfax, whom she mistakes as her employer. Jane notes that the handwriting is 'old-fashioned and rather uncertain, like that of an elderly lady', which is 'satisfactory'. She appears to have carefully examined the handwriting before drawing this conclusion, which suggests that she understands the potential risk of her action. There is a sense of relief when she concludes that an 'elderly lady' is her employer. Her list of three adjectives ('respectable, proper, en règle') emphasises this relief and the importance of respectability.

Etiquette

Mr Rochester frequently ignores the rules of etiquette (strict rules about how to speak to the opposite sex) when he talks to Jane. For example, when she meets him in chapter 13 for the second time, he speaks 'gruffly' and in an 'abrupt', direct manner, not following the normal rules of politeness. A Victorian lady might have been offended by this, but his manner puts Jane at ease. She says a 'finished politeness would probably have confused me', and so his way of speaking gives her 'the advantage'. By 'advantage', she means that she is in control. This has connotations of a competition, introducing the theme of roles between men and women. Finally, Mr Rochester breaking the rules of etiquette foreshadows his later defiance of social conventions when he attempts the bigamous marriage.

Traditionally, men initiated conversations; Mr Rochester directs the conversation and questions Jane in chapter 13, so we see that he is a man used to having power. Jane's responses to Mr Rochester, on the other hand, do not always conform to gender expectations. Wollstonecraft believed that women were taught to be subordinate, and this resulted in weakness and artificiality because women wanted to please other people. In chapter 14, Mr Rochester orders Jane to 'speak' and she refuses, responding with 'not a very complacent or submissive smile'. She is offended by his order and will not allow him to dominate her completely. Jane is not going to 'talk for the mere sake of talking and showing off', conveying a feminist attitude towards the gender role expectations of the time. Through Jane, Brontë criticises women who talk for the sake of it and have nothing interesting or intelligent to say.

In conversation with Mr Rochester, Jane is sometimes blunt to the point of rudeness, and her behaviour contrasts with that of Céline Varens, who in the novel's structure serves as Jane's foil. For example, Mr Rochester asks Jane if she thinks him 'handsome' and she bluntly replies 'No, Sir'. Her response could hardly be more different from Céline's who, Mr Rochester tells Jane, would 'launch out into fervent admiration' of him and 'The contrast struck' him. Jane's unconventional directness is part of her attraction.

In Victorian times, some subjects were not mentioned in front of young unmarried women. Contemporary readers would have been shocked by Mr Rochester telling Jane in chapter 15 about his affair with Céline Varens: not only would readers have been scandalised by the subject matter, but also the fact that he is crossing boundaries of class and convention. He uses his spiritual connection with Jane to justify his confidences, saying that she has a 'peculiar' and 'unique' mind that 'would not take harm' from him. He hopes that she will 'refresh' him and make him a better man. The adjectives to describe her mind show that in his eyes she is different to other women and emphasise that he is addressing her on a spiritual level. His desire for her to 'refresh' him demonstrates his recognition of her strength of character and suggests that she can heal him and teach him better ways. Perhaps Brontë is implying that some women should not be sheltered like children.

Another rule of etiquette was that a young unmarried lady should be chaperoned at all times and certainly never left alone with a single man. Contemporary readers would have been shocked by Jane walking alone in the garden with Mr Rochester after she has helped Mr Mason. This would have been very dangerous for Jane as it is just before 'sunrise'—in effect, at night. If anyone had seen them, this would have ruined Jane's reputation.

The risk to a woman's reputation is hinted at when Mr Rochester is reluctant to allow Jane to leave his bedroom after the fire. She notes a 'strange energy was in his voice, strange fire in his look', which symbolises his growing passion for her that she does not completely understand because of her inexperience. Nevertheless, she is aware of impropriety (doing wrong) and says that she is 'cold', which contrasts with the 'fire in his look', demonstrating that she is able to control herself. It is only when she says that she can hear Mrs Fairfax—the consequences of being found in her employer's bedroom are implied—that he allows her to leave.

Differences between the Sexes

In Victorian times, there were strong beliefs about the perceived differences between the sexes. Men were regarded as dominant and rational while women were seen as weak and subservient, prone to hysteria and incapable of rational thought. This is one reason why the Brontës published their novels under male pseudonyms. In 1792, Mary Wollstonecraft published 'A Vindication of the Rights of Woman', which challenged attitudes towards women and argued that, through education, women were equally capable of rational thought. While modern views are different, it is worth pointing out that we have not wholly escaped from these Victorian attitudes.

A contemporary stereotype was that women were so fragile and emotional that they would faint at the sight of blood (fainting is reflected in many gothic novels of the time such as Ann Radcliffe's 'The Mysteries of Udolpho'). This helps the modern reader to understand why Mr Rochester asks Jane if she turns 'sick at the sight of blood' in chapter 20. By helping him and not fainting, she takes an active more conventionally male role. Brontë is therefore challenging contemporary views about women and encouraging the reader to examine Mr Rochester's prejudices.

Mr Rochester exploits the stereotype of the nervous woman when Jane tells him about the dreams she had before the visit of the 'Vampyre', who rips her wedding veil in two. He states that Jane's dreams are the product of an 'over-stimulated brain' and blames her 'nerves'. He suggests that she shares 'Adèle's little bed' and locks the door of the 'nursery', protecting her as if she is a child, thereby emphasising her inferior status. Interestingly, we later learn that Bertha did bite her brother, Mr Mason, and she is metaphorically draining the life out of Mr Rochester. The older Jane narrating the story deliberately withholds the truth about Bertha from us, choosing instead to exploit traditional gender stereotypes. By reporting Jane and Mr Rochester's 'Vampyre' conversation, she therefore develops suspense.

From the beginning of the novel, Brontë challenges contemporary beliefs about males being the superior sex through her depiction of John Reed. He is fat ('large and stout') because he 'gorged' himself at meal times. Gluttony of course is one of the seven deadly sins. He 'bullied and punished' Jane continually. We see the foolishness of his mother who, because of his gender, indulges him and is 'blind and deaf' to his tyrannical, bullying ways. His eventual suicide, the consequence of his drinking, gambling and debts, encourages the reader to challenge the perception of his simple male superiority.

Jane as a young girl is expected to be passive. Brontë shows the reader that she rejects contemporary gender roles by fighting back against John Reed in 'fury' and 'passion'. This can also be seen when she is taken to the red-room and, in 'a moment's mutiny', resists 'like a rebel slave'. The slave imagery could be a metaphor for women being imprisoned by the gender expectations of the time. Wollstonecraft accused writers like Rousseau of wanting women to be virtual slaves. She believed that educated girls would have the tools to fight back against male oppression. The young Jane's rebelliousness against her 'slavery' foreshadows her ability to make active decisions about her life after receiving her 'excellent' education at Lowood.

We see Miss Temple struggling to conform to contemporary expectations of the submissive female role at Lowood School when Mr Brocklehurst orders her to let the children go hungry. Miss Temple 'gazed straight before her, and her face, naturally pale as marble, appeared to be assuming also the coldness and fixity of that material'. The cold, pale, stone imagery suggests that she is working hard to control her emotions, but the description of 'her mouth' which 'would have required a sculptor's chisel to open it' might be a metaphor for the oppression of women, who were not expected to argue back. Moreover, when Mr Brocklehurst orders the girls' top-knots to be cut off, 'Miss Temple seemed to remonstrate' but her voice is not heard, perhaps representing the voices of many women of the time. Miss Temple fails to challenge Mr Brocklehurst, so this is different from what we know of Jane's character.

Jane challenges the contemporary belief that older, experienced men are necessarily superior to younger, less experienced women. She tells Mr Rochester 'I don't think, sir, you have a right to command me, merely because you are older than I, or because you have seen more of the world than I have; your claim to superiority depends on the use you have made of your time and experience'. The educated Jane thinks and judges for herself; assessing the hypocritical Mr Brocklehurst and the poor behaviour of the Reeds, she refuses to take people at face value. Brontë might also be encouraging her readers not to take people, especially men, at face value.

Finally, Jane challenges conventions when she initiates a conversation with St. John about Rosamond: a 'surprised expression crossed his face. He had not imagined that a woman would dare to speak so to a man'. The verb 'dare' emphasises the gulf between men and women at that time. It suggests that women were naturally timid and afraid of men. Jane, however, when talking to 'strong, discreet, and refined minds, whether male or female', likes to move beyond 'conventional reserve'. This could emphasise Brontë's belief that people should be able to interact on a serious level with like-minded others, regardless of their gender.

The Importance of Looks

The writer and thinker Mary Wollstonecraft strongly criticised contemporary beliefs that a female's looks were the most important thing about her. The servant Miss Abbot comments in chapter 3 that, if Jane were a 'nice, pretty child', she might feel sorry for her, 'but one really cannot care for such a little toad as that'. She equates prettiness with goodness, as the adjective 'nice' is juxtaposed with 'pretty'. The use of 'toad' implies that Jane is not only ugly, but repulsive and possibly wicked. This reflects the contemporary belief attacked by Wollstonecraft that good looks helped to define a girl's or a woman's position in society. Blanche Ingram develops this idea when she says 'an ugly woman is a blot on the fair face of creation'. We have already seen that it is ironic that the 'beautiful Blanche' is in fact a thoroughly unpleasant person and certainly not 'nice'. By making her physically beautiful but extremely unpleasant, Brontë is encouraging her readers to question contemporary beliefs about judging women by their appearances, and beauty implying goodness.

Jane is keenly aware of her lack of conventional beauty. In chapter 11, on her first morning at Thornfield, she says 'I felt it a misfortune that I was so little, so pale, and had features so irregular and so marked.' The repetition of 'so' and the very careful choice of adjectives emphasise her sadness about being plain. Perhaps she wishes to be more attractive to make a good impression. However, at least Jane has her intelligence and education to fall back on: these—rather than her looks—will help her to make her way in life.

Married Women's Rights

Brontë lived in a patriarchal society in which women's rights were limited. The moment a woman married, she became the property of her husband. Because women were not regarded in the eyes of the law as separate entities from their husbands, they did not have the right to vote. In addition, they were not allowed to own property and, if they worked, their earnings were the property of their husbands. Marriage, which tended to be for life, was therefore a huge financial as well as emotional risk for women.

Jane feels this keenly when Mr Rochester in chapter 24 says 'I will myself put the diamond chain round your neck'. This conversation, which takes place after Jane has accepted his proposal, emphasises the difference between the couple. Mr Rochester wants to shower her with jewels; Jane feels uncomfortable. The conversation symbolises their feelings about power in a relationship. The 'diamond chain' has connotations of prisoners in chains and gilded cages. It also reminds us of the slave imagery that Jane uses (see *Differences between the Sexes*, above). It emphasises that, no matter how pretty and expensive the diamonds, Jane will be the legal property of her husband. When she insists that she is a 'plain, Quakerish governess', she is holding onto her identity, not wanting to be chained down. She clearly has concerns about relinquishing her independence when she marries. Her desire for independence within the relationship would have been regarded as unwomanly and against God's will by some contemporary readers.

In chapter 34, we see how marriage affects the balance of power within a relationship. Accompanying St. John to India as a 'fellow-soldier' or friend, Jane would retain her independent identity; as his wife, she would be completely under his control. She would become, as St. John says, 'part of' him, 'always restrained, and always checked'. This is highly disturbing imagery, as it suggests Jane would be a prisoner. There is no suggestion that the marriage would be between spiritual equals: Jane would be a slave, her identity absorbed into St. John's, with the 'imprisoned flame' of passion inside her, consuming her from within. Jane is aware that St. John 'prizes' her 'as a soldier would a good weapon'. This war imagery reflects his attitude towards his missionary work, which has nothing to do with changing hearts and minds, and has more to do with forcing people into submission. He reduces Jane to the status of a weapon in war, to be used by him. In marriage, his 'measured warrior-march' would 'trample' Jane down and erase her identity completely. This war imagery perhaps symbolises a war between the sexes and again suggests that women have everything to lose upon marriage.

Trapped in Roles

Brontë's opinions (also seen in her novel 'Shirley') about the restricted lives that women lead echo Wollstonecraft's. Using Jane as her mouthpiece, Brontë explains how women are denied their potential in society by being confined to the home:

> Women are supposed to be very calm generally: but women feel just as men feel; they need exercise for their faculties, and a field for their efforts, as much as their brothers do; they suffer from too rigid a restraint, too absolute a stagnation, precisely as men would suffer; and it is narrow-minded in their more privileged fellow-creatures to say that they ought to confine themselves to making puddings and knitting stockings, to playing on the piano and embroidering bags. It is thoughtless to condemn them, or laugh at them, if they seek to do more or learn more than custom has pronounced necessary for their sex.

These words illustrate just how far middle- and upper-class women were imprisoned within their homes because equal opportunities in education and work did not exist. Jane is fortunate because an education provides her with a means to earn her own living although her career options are limited (see *Theme and Context: Education*). Throughout the novel, Jane is imprisoned in other ways: she needs to escape Mr Brocklehurst's hypocritical views, Mr Rochester's passion without restraint, and St. John's restraint without passion.

In 'The Madwoman in the Attic', an early classic of feminist criticism published in 1979, authors Gilbert and Gubar state that nineteenth century writers like Brontë could only make female characters angels or monsters because of the gender expectations of the time. Jane's angelic restraint therefore contrasts with Bertha Rochester's madness, and the two women serve as foils to each other.

Other critics argue that there are parallels between Jane, the angry child imprisoned in the red-room, and Bertha, the angry woman imprisoned in the attic. When Bertha puts Jane's veil on her head and turns to the 'mirror', Jane sees Bertha's face in its 'reflection' for the first time. Normally, a person would expect to see their own reflection first, so perhaps Brontë is suggesting that Bertha is an extension of Jane. Bertha might therefore symbolise what Jane might have become, had she not learnt to control her passions.

Further evidence for this theory can be seen in one of Jane's dreams in which there is a child 'too young and feeble to walk'. This child could symbolise Jane's fears about not being able to create an independent role for herself within marriage. Bertha, on the other hand, might represent Jane's anxiety about voicing her fear and anger. The implication is that if Jane gives vent to her feelings, she will end up like Bertha, full of rage.

There is also a theory that Bertha Rochester symbolises Brontë's anxieties about marriage and its destructive potential. By Victorian standards, Brontë married very late in life at the age of thirty-eight, which might suggest a reluctance to marry when she was younger. The potential of a marriage to destroy a woman's identity can be seen in chapter 26 when Jane describes Bertha as an animal:

> *What it was, whether beast or human being, one could not, at first sight, tell: it grovelled, seemingly, on all fours; it snatched and growled like some strange wild animal: but it was covered with clothing, and a quantity of dark, grizzled hair, wild as a mane, hid its head and face.*

The animal imagery could symbolise that not only has Bertha has been stripped of her identity, but that she has also been stripped of her humanity. Brontë might be implying that women who do not conform to expected behavioural standards lose their identities and become, as Gilbert and Gubar would say, monsters. The use of animal imagery suggests a loss of self-control, which is demonstrated when Bertha attacks Mr Rochester and Mr Mason. However, she is not seen to attack anyone else. This might imply that, despite being depicted as a monster, she is still capable of rational thought, as she could be blaming the men for locking her away. Bertha could therefore be the external symbol of Brontë's internal frustrations about being trapped in a patriarchal society.

There have been many other interpretations of Bertha's character, which include:

- She symbolises the consequences of being restricted in a Victorian marriage. Bertha was 'intemperate and unchaste', choosing her sexual partners, which was unacceptable behaviour for a nineteenth-century English wife. Perhaps she is locked away because of her 'vices 'rather than because she is 'infirm in mind'. If this is the case, locking her up might have *caused* her madness.
- Bertha's promiscuousness could be her way of rebelling against her lack of freedom in marriage. Being legally regarded as the property of her husband might have affected her mental and emotional health. When Bertha tears Jane's wedding veil in half, this could symbolise her rebellion against the institution of marriage.
- Bertha's mother is a 'Creole'. Bertha is therefore mixed race. By escaping imprisonment and trying to burn Mr Rochester in his bed, she might symbolise the British Empire's anxieties about controlling its subjects, who could rise at any time to rebel against cultural and economic exploitation by their imperial masters.

Finally, it is worth noting that Bertha is as big as Mr Rochester ('in stature almost equalling her husband') and that he has to physically fight her to control her. Perhaps Brontë is showing that women can defy gender stereotyping and challenge their allotted role in society—and that this is an issue that will not easily go away.

Sex Before Marriage

Victorian gentlemen would expect to marry virgins, so it was the norm (but not the rule) for middle- and upper-class women to refrain from sex before marriage. We see in the novel the double standards of the time, as Mr Rochester has had at least three mistresses ('Céline, Giacinta, and Clara'). It was well understood that middle- and upper-class men were free to indulge in premarital sex with partners from all ranks in society, including servants and prostitutes.

Mr Rochester's lack of respect for mistresses can be seen when he says 'Hiring a mistress is the next worse thing to buying a slave: both are often by nature, and always by position, inferior: and to live familiarly with inferiors is degrading'. The offensive (as we would understand it today) attitude and imagery expressed in these words clearly demonstrate that mistresses can be discarded at will because they are never in a position of equality. If Jane were to become his mistress, Mr Rochester would therefore have full power over her, but she would have none of the legal protection of a wife. As well as ruining her reputation, Jane is aware that becoming his mistress would be 'wicked' in the eyes of God; this links back to the earlier slave imagery, as she would be spiritually as well as emotionally imprisoned.

Even engaged couples were encouraged not to indulge in premarital sex. After Jane accepts Mr Rochester's hand in marriage, Mrs Fairfax advises her to keep Mr Rochester at a distance: 'distrust yourself as well as him. Gentlemen in his station are not accustomed to marry their governesses'. Jane follows this advice, which works to her advantage when she discovers that he is already married; otherwise, her reputation and status in society would have been completely ruined, despite her being blameless.

Divorce

During Brontë's lifetime, The Church of England managed divorce cases. Consequently, Mr Rochester would not have been allowed to divorce his insane wife because a divorce needed to be agreed by both parties. Bertha could not agree to this because of her madness, which in itself was not considered legitimate grounds for divorce. This changed in 1857 (three years after Brontë's death and ten years after the publication of 'Jane Eyre') with the Matrimonial Causes Act, which gave civil courts the power to grant divorces; however, only men could obtain a divorce, and this was on the grounds of adultery.

In the game of charades in chapter 18, Blanche and Mr Rochester enact a 'pantomime of a marriage' as the first part of the answer, 'Bridewell'. Bridewell (a pun on the words 'bride' and 'well' and also the name of a famous prison of the time) symbolises the fact that Mr Rochester is imprisoned in his loveless marriage. The 'pantomime' foreshadows other sham weddings: the attempt at the bigamous wedding on Jane's wedding day; and the revelation of Mr Rochester's dysfunctional marriage to Bertha. He is confined by a 'chain' and his wrists are 'in fetters', linking marriage to imprisonment, with no hope of release.

When Mr Rochester tells Jane that he wants to marry her, her response ('Your bride stands between us') is ironic. She is talking about Blanche Ingram; she does not know that he already has another wife hidden away—a wife who is mad. Mr Rochester calls Jane his 'equal' and 'likeness'. Perhaps he thinks that they are similar because they are not conventionally handsome or beautiful. He might also be referring to their spiritual and emotional connection, or mutual sexual attraction. He tries to justify his attempted marriage to Jane later, by saying that Bertha is not his 'likeness' so she cannot be his wife—even though the law says otherwise. He attempts to defend his attempted bigamous marriage to Jane, which would be against the laws of society and God.

Mr Rochester compares Jane to Bertha and appeals to Mr Mason and Mr Briggs, saying 'Compare these clear eyes with the red balls yonder—this face with that mask—this form with that bulk'. By comparing the women, Mr Rochester is appealing for everyone's sympathy. His comparison of the two women encourages the reader to empathise with Mr Rochester (although some might say the comparisons are insensitive); this also encourages the reader to consider and perhaps criticise the laws of divorce.

Inversion of Roles

The inversion of gender roles and relations is explored in the novel. For example, in chapter 12, the traditional dominant male and passive female roles appear to be inverted when Jane meets Mr Rochester for the first time. Although some might say that Mr Rochester orders Jane about and that she attempts to nurse him (a traditional, subservient role which sees her literally used as a support), others might interpret this differently. For example, Jane takes a dominant role when she asserts 'I cannot think of leaving you…till I see you are fit to mount your horse' and, when she leaves him to resume her walk to Hay, she is 'pleased to have done something' as she 'was weary of an existence all passive', echoing Wollstonecraft's view that it is not natural for women to be inactive. The fact that Mr Rochester has 'a sprain' and needs Jane's help might alternatively be interpreted as him being dependent on her. This is significant because it could foreshadow his dependence upon Jane for help at key moments in the Thornfield chapters (such as rescuing him from the fire or helping him with Mr Mason) and later in the Ferndean chapters. The encounter between Jane and Mr Rochester and their inverted gender roles therefore helps to establish the couple's relationship as equals.

Jane also takes the active male role when she declares her love to Mr Rochester at Thornfield and, in unusual behaviour for a contemporary woman, demands respect and equality:

> Do you think, because I am poor, obscure, plain and little, I am soulless and heartless? You think wrong! - I have as much soul as you, - and full as much heart! And if God had gifted me with some beauty and much wealth, I should have made it as hard for you to leave me, as it is now for me to leave you!

Jane's use of exclamations demonstrates her passion and feelings for Mr Rochester, prompting him to propose to her. She does not therefore passively accept the circumstances that life throws at her.

Gender Relations at Ferndean

At Ferndean, there is symbolism when Jane takes a tray of 'water' and 'candles' to Mr Rochester. A straightforward interpretation is that this represents Jane accepting the traditional subservient female role; however, in her approach to Rochester, 'the water spilt from the glass'. It spills because she is emotional and her hands are shaking; the spilt water might also symbolise Jane moving on from her role of a dependent (she is no longer restricted like water in a glass) and finding a new place for herself in the world. The 'candles' on the tray might symbolise that Jane is guiding Mr Rochester into a brighter future. Alternatively, he has them brought in every night despite being unable to see, so they might represent his hope. Light also has connotations of the light of God, suggesting the possibility of forgiveness for sins.

Jane meets Mr Rochester on greater terms of equality because of her inheritance. One of the first things she says is: 'I am independent, sir, as well as rich: I am my own mistress'. This time, Mr Rochester accepts Jane as she is and does not try to change her like he did at Thornfield when she objected to being dressed like a 'doll'. At Ferndean, Mr Rochester says that 'fine clothes and jewels' are 'not worth a fillip' (the flick of a finger), indicating that he has come to a deeper understanding of life and, ironically now that he is blind, appreciates that a woman should not be judged solely by her appearance.

Jane stresses her independent status by deliberately teasing Mr Rochester about St. John. The differences between the two men, who serve as foils, is obvious when she describes St. John as a 'handsome man: tall, fair, with blue eyes, and a Grecian profile'. This contrasts with Mr Rochester, whom Jane agrees is 'hideous'! He calls himself 'a real blacksmith, brown, broad-shouldered: and blind and lame into the bargain'. The classically handsome St. John is almost too good to be true while we associate Mr Rochester the 'blacksmith' with fire and passion. Moreover, Brontë appears to be carefully evoking the image of Hephaestus, the lame blacksmith of Olympus, who married Athene, the Greek goddess of wisdom. This suggests that Jane identifies herself with Athene, reminding the reader that the novel is a Bildungsroman with its focus on Jane's physical and spiritual development. Her responses to her internal and external conflicts throughout her life have combined to develop her sense of self and make her a wiser, stronger person.

Another interesting image at Ferndean is that of Mr Rochester's 'shaggy black mane' of hair that Jane tries to comb. This could be an allusion to the Biblical story of Samson, who was given immense strength by God. His lover Delilah is bribed by his enemies to unearth the secret of his strength. When she learns that it is his long hair, she has her servant shave it off when he is asleep and so he loses all his strength. Consequently, He is captured by his enemies, who blind him. We therefore have the image of Jane seeing herself as the dominant person in the relationship and holding power over the blind Mr Rochester.

Mr Rochester's eyes have a symbolic function in the couple's relationship. In chapter 36, we learn that he has lost one eye and gone 'blind' in the other. The loss of his sight might symbolise his loss of pride and power, again reminding us of Samson. (He later tells Jane, 'I was proud of my strength'). It might also represent divine retribution—a punishment from God for attempting a bigamous marriage. At the end of chapter 37, Jane describes herself as his 'prop and guide'. He leans on her when she guides him into the wood, as he did when he came off his horse at the beginning of their relationship; as his 'guide', she is more dominant. Emotionally, he needs her, as she 'cheers' his 'withered heart' and 'puts life into it', but Mr Rochester is dependent upon Jane in a more practical way: 'I was then his vision'. As his eyes symbolise his power, this power is now in Jane's hands. Eventually, he 'recovered the sight of that one eye', which could suggest the mercy of God and possible forgiveness for his sins. It might also indicate that their relationship has become more equal. We therefore learn from Jane that is possible to give and take in a loving relationship and still have a degree of intellectual and emotional independence.

One of the most famous lines in literature is at the end of the novel when Jane announces 'Reader, I married him'. Jane's use of the active 'I married him' instead of the passive 'he married me' reflects her dominance in the relationship.

The novel, in the view of some feminist critics, seems to suggest that only way a woman can be happy is through marriage. This is emphasised when we learn that Jane's cousins Diana and Mary also marry and live happily ever after. However, Brontë seems to be saying that, despite the prejudices against women and the constraints of social class, it might still be possible for a woman to find and marry her spiritual equal. The description in chapter 38 of Jane and Mr Rochester's marriage appears to be of perfect equality. She says that no 'woman was ever nearer to her mate than I am: ever more absolutely bone of his bone and flesh of his flesh'. The novel has been about Jane developing into an independent person, and her earlier fears of losing her individuality in marriage have proven to be unfounded.

Theme and Context: Passion versus Restraint

The thematic conflict between passion and restraint can be seen with hot and cold imagery within the novel. At Gateshead, for example, the young Jane loses her temper with Mrs Reed, who has lied about her to Mr Brocklehurst. Mrs. Reed's 'eye of ice' symbolising a cold heart and a lack of compassion looks 'freezingly' at Jane. This contrasts with Jane's description of herself as a 'ridge of lighted heath, alive, glancing, devouring'. This triplet suggests life, movement and passion. We have a sense of wildness as she enjoys rebelling against the tyranny of her aunt. Like fire, Jane is unable to control herself.

The themes are also developed through the use of contrasting characters and situations. At Lowood School in chapter 5, Miss Scatcherd punishes Helen Burns, and Jane notices that Helen 'looks as if she were thinking of something beyond her punishment—beyond her situation'. Helen, like the orphan in Bessie's ballad in chapter 3, is restraining her passions by ignoring her present problems and focusing on the spiritual. Helen's character is Christ-like as she meekly accepts unfair punishments. This contrasts with Jane's rebellious and passionate attitude: as we saw at Gateshead, she would 'strike back again very hard' in the face of injustice. Therefore, while Helen exercises self-restraint and focuses on heaven, Jane indulges her passions.

An important moment in Jane's development is when she manages to control her passions. After Mr Brocklehurst makes her stand on a stool for the rest of the day, Helen walks past and the 'strange light' in her eyes sends an 'extraordinary sensation' through Jane. We have connotations of the light of God shining through her eyes, suggesting that there is comfort in God. Jane compares Helen to a 'hero' and herself to a 'slave or victim' to whom Helen has 'imparted strength'. This slave imagery reminds the reader of the earlier slave imagery when Jane was being taken to the red-room. There was no 'hero' then, but now Jane has a role model and hope. She is inspired by Helen to control her 'rising hysteria', and this marks a significant moment in her development.

In chapter 8, we see that Helen and Miss Temple continue to constructively influence Jane's ability to control her passions. When she describes her life at Gateshead to Miss Temple, Jane resolves to be 'moderate' with her language, to reflect and 'arrange' her thoughts before speaking. She then tells her story in a 'restrained and simplified' way, noting that, as a result, it sounds 'more credible'. This is the first time that we see Jane control her emotions by thinking before speaking. For the first time in her life, she has the positive role models of Helen and Miss Temple, who are both rational, educated females.

The limit to which passion can be restrained by a positive role model is seen, however, when Miss Temple marries and leaves. Jane recognises Miss Temple's influence on her character when she says 'I believed I was content: to the eyes of others, usually even to my own, I appeared a disciplined and subdued character'. The adjectives 'disciplined and subdued' reflect the subordinate, self-controlled behaviour expected of young women at the time. The verb 'appeared', however, implies that this was not the reality, even when Miss Temple was at Lowood. After Miss Temple leaves, Jane realises that she 'borrowed' these emotions and that she feels the 'stirring of old emotions'. Pathetic fallacy reflects her feelings when she looks out of her window at the 'remote' and 'blue peaks' of the mountains. They symbolise her desire to leave and scale new heights, which appear to be beautiful and remote. Jane has learnt to control her feelings in social situations, but her restless, passionate nature remains.

In chapter 23, the colour red is used in a pathetic fallacy to symbolise the couple's passion before Mr Rochester proposes: the sky is 'burning with the light of red jewel and furnace flame at one point'. The imagery suggests that their beautiful and passionate love is as natural as the elements. However, red also symbolises anger and could foreshadow divine disapproval of their union.

The use of fire as an image of passion is also seen in chapter 15 when Bertha Rochester attempts to burn Mr Rochester in his bed. The personified imagery of 'tongues of flame' is sensual, and the burning bed symbolises his uncontrollable past passions: he must live with their consequences. Connected to this, the lit candle that Jane finds outside Mr Rochester's bedroom symbolises Bertha's passions, which can flare up at any moment. This foreshadows her uncontrollable madness and passion when she sets fire to Thornfield Hall.

Moreover, fire serves as a plot or structural device in the following instance: despite Jane believing that Grace Poole started the bedroom fire, the servant behaves normally the next day. The reader therefore shares Jane's suspicion that 'somebody has plotted something', so the mystery and danger are developed. This deception, linked with Mr Rochester's refusal to tell Jane about the cause of the fire, symbolises his greater deception when concealing the truth about Bertha.

The red motif continues in chapter 18 when Mr Rochester disguises himself as a gypsy woman. Mr Rochester's 'red cloak', like the red-room and fire, connotes passion. The cloak therefore symbolises his feelings towards Jane; however, the upper-class Mr Rochester in disguise as a female is vulnerable and cannot tell Jane his feelings towards her. Consequently, the 'hat-brim partially shaded her face', symbolising not only that he is concealing his identity but also that he is hiding his feelings. The cloak and hat together form a barrier to Jane who, at this stage of the story, cannot see into his heart.

Bronte employs other symbols in the novel's examination of the battle between passion and restraint. In chapter 27, light imagery is used to suggest that Mr Rochester's passions are his downfall. He describes his first meeting with Bertha: he was 'dazzled, stimulated: my senses were excited; and being ignorant, raw, and inexperienced, I thought I loved her'. The adjective 'dazzled' suggests that his passion for Bertha was so strong that it blinded him while 'stimulated' and 'excited' suggest a loss of control. This is balanced with the three adjectives 'ignorant, raw, and inexperienced' as if he is depicting himself as a victim. This will make the reader feel sympathetic or cynical about his depiction of himself.

Whilst Mr Rochester struggles to control his passions, Jane is able to control hers. She employs cold, hard imagery when thinking about her own state of mind: she 'must be ice and rock to him'. This contrasts greatly with Mr Rochester's own passion that he struggles to control. He is in a 'fury' and he seems to 'devour' Jane with his 'flaming glance'. It is almost as if he is transformed into a devil trying to lead Jane into temptation. In comparison, Jane controls her passions ('only an idiot…would have succumbed now'), and she extracts herself from the situation by leaving the room. Her 'ice and rock' restraint foreshadows her later encounter with St. John who is the very embodiment of icy behaviour.

The extent of Jane's struggles with her passions is shown through the literary device of personification when she decides to leave Thornfield Hall: 'Conscience, turned tyrant, held Passion by the throat'. The personification of her conscience physically dominating her passion vividly reveals her powerful emotional struggles. By choosing to leave Mr Rochester, Jane rejects a passion without self-restraint: her conscience tells her she should value her self-respect and virtue more than her passionate love for Mr Rochester.

Understanding that moral integrity is more important than her passion for Mr Rochester, she comments: 'The more solitary, the more friendless, the more unsustained I am, the more I will respect myself. I will keep the law given by God'. She therefore places the laws of God over her desires. She now needs time to heal and to re-establish her identity. By choosing to take very little with her, she will also literally and symbolically need to recreate herself from nothing.

St. John Rivers, who symbolises self-restraint, serves as a foil to Mr Rochester. In chapter 29, we learn that he is classically handsome with a 'Greek face' and 'an Athenian mouth and chin'. Unlike Mr Rochester, his 'eyes were large and blue, with brown lashes; his high forehead, colourless as ivory, was partially streaked over by careless locks of fair hair'. The appearance of this blue-eyed, fair-haired, classically handsome pastor would, to Victorian eyes, reflect is goodness as a man of God. He controls his emotions, however, and Jane senses his 'reserve', noting that he speaks 'coolly'. These characteristics contrast with Mr Rochester's 'passion'.

To better compare St. John with Mr Rochester, the reader needs to see the former reject passionate love—something that Mr Rochester would never do. St. John tells Jane 'I love Rosamond Oliver so wildly'. The adverb 'wildly' indicates a desire to lose himself in his passion, yet by describing himself as a 'cold hard man', he suppresses his love for Rosamond, dismissing it as 'human weakness'. His 'suffering and sacrifice' are at a great cost: St. John says that Rosamond means 'Rose of the World' so, with this comparison to a beautiful flower, she represents nature. He wishes to reject earthly love and passion, embodied in Rosamond. Therefore, while Mr Rochester allows his passions to rule his behaviour, we see the opposite extreme in the character of St. John.

Jane considers St. John's proposal before rejecting it, stating 'he asks me to be his wife, and has no more of a husband's heart for me than that frowning giant of a rock'. The 'frowning giant of a rock' imagery suggests the immensity of his dispassionate, hard heart. Like a rock, he is immovable, implying that he will never love Jane. Perhaps he is also 'frowning' because he would be constantly judging her and trying to change her.

This would not be a marriage between two spiritual equals. Jane's contrasting attitude to marriage can be seen with the alliteration of 'husband's heart', with the soft -h suggesting a desire for tenderness and passion.

As his character develops, we associate St. John more and more with ice and snow imagery to symbolise self-restraint. In chapter 33, he arrives at Jane's cottage from a 'tempest' of 'snow', which covers his boots and cloak, symbolising the dominance of self-restraint over earthly passion. He is literally coldness personified. He tells Jane 'I am cold: no fervour infects me', indicating that he has completely supressed his passion for earthly love. The contrast between him and Jane is evident when she replies that she is 'hot, and fire dissolves ice'. We see at this stage that they will never be compatible as husband and wife; this foreshadows her later rejection of him. The only 'fire' that will dissolve him is the fire of his religious zeal.

The contrasting attitudes between Jane and St. John are developed by Brontë when Jane learns that the solicitor Mr Briggs is looking for her. Passion and feeling dominate Jane, who is more concerned with Mr Rochester ('How and where is he? What is he doing? Is he well?') while St. John replies 'you forget essential points in pursuing trifles: you do not inquire why Mr. Briggs sought after you—what he wanted with you'. Being a dispassionate man, he does not understand Jane. This contrast between the two develops when Jane learns that she is related to the Rivers siblings. She shows more excitement about this than about inheriting the money. When she exclaims 'I am glad!', St. John comments 'You were serious when I told you you had got a fortune; and now, for a matter of no moment, you are excited'. Not being interested in worldly issues, he considers their family relationship 'a matter of no moment'. This is a shocking response. Not only does it reveal his inability to understand Jane but, as a man of God he shows a remarkable inability to understand hearts and minds. This foreshadows his later attitude of converting people with his missionary work—they must bend to his will.

Stone imagery is added to the ice imagery to symbolise St. John's restraint and inflexible will. Jane compares him to a 'cold cumbrous column' and 'white stone'. St. John, who is good at heart, is associated more and more with the colour white (unlike Mr Brocklehurst who, a 'black pillar', is wicked at heart). Stone is cold and hard and, in chapter 35, St. John's coldness develops into inhumanity when Jane rejects his offer of marriage. He is 'no longer flesh, but marble, his eye is 'a cold, bright, blue gem' and his heart is 'stone or metal'. These are beautiful but cold and hard elements, which create quite a frightening image. They combine to create a 'refined, lingering torture' for Jane, and she asks if we know:

> ...what terror those cold people can put into the ice of their questions? how much of the fall of the avalanche is in their anger? of the breaking up of the frozen sea in their displeasure?

This imagery illustrates the power of his will and his ability to dominate others. The imagery of 'ice', 'avalanche' and 'frozen sea' represents nature on a large scale and suggests Jane's hopelessness: as a mere human, she is unable to stop an avalanche or break up a frozen sea. This imagery not only emphasises the difference between St.

John and Jane, but it creates tension for the reader, who worries that Jane will eventually submit to his will.

The climax of the Moor House chapters is when Jane almost agrees to marry St. John and comes very close to allowing her passions to be oppressed in a loveless marriage. She is saved by divine intervention, which will be discussed below. Consequently, Jane rejects judgement without passion.

Theme and Context: The Supernatural

Structural Importance

The supernatural plays an important role in the thematic structure of the novel. Every time that Jane has a supernatural experience, it heralds a significant change in her life, often foreshadowing the future.

Her first experience of a supernatural event is when in chapter 2 she is locked in the red-room, sees a 'light' and believes it to be the 'ghost' of her dead uncle. This triggers her hysteria and blackout, the subsequent visit from Mr Lloyd, and Jane's departure to Lowood. It is the first introduction of the supernatural, and it sets the tone for future events.

The next supernatural experience is hinted at in chapter 10 when, bored at Lowood, Jane says a 'kind fairy' suggests that she advertise for a new position. The 'kind fairy' is probably a metaphor for Jane having a good idea, but it could also be interpreted as a supernatural intervention, which results in her subsequent departure from Lowood and employment at Thornfield Hall.

Upon her return to Thornfield Hall after her visit to Gateshead, Jane believes that Mr Rochester will marry Blanche. The supernatural continues to look after her interests when Jane says 'a 'voice' was 'warning' her of 'near separation and coming grief'. There is irony, however, as the warning 'voice' is likely to be referring to events on her own wedding day instead of Blanche Ingram. This misleads the reader, creating a greater shock when the reader discovers that Mr Rochester is already married.

Upon learning that Mr Rochester is married, Jane is once more prompted to act by the 'voice within', which tells her to 'Leave Thornfield at once'. (Is this the same voice as the 'kind fairy', above?) Jane also dreams of her mother, who whispers 'My daughter, flee temptation'. These voices prompt her to leave Thornfield Hall, triggering the next phase of her life, in which she needs to atone for the sin of placing Mr Rochester above God before she can be forgiven and find happiness. These other-worldly voices prompt her to reflect, heal and rebuild her life. By the end of the subsequent Moor House chapters, she will be an independent woman: her fortune, her desirability as a wife, and her self-confidence are very greatly enhanced. Indeed, so desirable has she become that Mr Rochester is jealous when he hears about St. John.

Perhaps the strongest supernatural experience that Jane has is when she almost agrees to marry St. John but is saved by divine intervention: Jane asks God to 'show' her the 'path', and he appears to answer her prayers with a psychic connection to Mr Rochester. This experience is a catalyst for her departure from Moor House. While there is an element of doubt about whether earlier supernatural occurrences were imaginary or real, this example of the couple's shared telepathic and spiritual bond is confirmed in chapter 37 by Mr Rochester. This suggests divine intervention: God intends them to be reunited. Brontë, as we know, was the daughter of a clergyman and, by confirming this shared psychic experience, she may feel she is providing evidence of God's existence.

Other-worldly and Mythic Imagery

Jane is often described in the novel using other-worldly imagery, which further links her to the supernatural theme. In chapter 2, she describes her reflection in the red-room mirror as 'one of the tiny phantoms, half fairy, half imp' from Bessie's stories, that comes out of 'lone, ferny dells and moors' and appears before 'belated travellers'. This foreshadows her first meeting with Mr Rochester in chapter 12 when he is travelling home at dusk. It also foreshadows Jane crossing the moors to Moor House. St. John, like Mr Rochester, is travelling home late.

Supernatural imagery pervades Jane and Mr Rochester's first meeting, creating a mythic element to their relationship. The setting of woods and the 'rising' moon that is 'waxing bright' evokes thoughts of the couple being under the influence of the supernatural world. Jane mistakes first Mr Rochester's horse and then his dog for 'Bessie's Gytrash', a supernatural 'spirit' which, according to northern England folklore, either leads travellers astray or guides lost travellers back to the right road. She is almost surprised when it does not look up to her 'with strange pretercanine eyes'. The idea of leading or misleading is a central linking image here: the dog's name is Pilot; he belongs to Mr Rochester; Mr Rochester attempts to mislead Jane into becoming his mistress. At the end of the Moor House chapters, Jane will somehow psychically hear Mr Rochester's voice guiding her back to him. The Gytrash imagery therefore enables us to understand Jane and Mr Rochester's first meeting on a mythical level, and the symbolism of the Gytrash foreshadows future events.

The idea of their meeting having fairy tale elements makes their relationship special: it is as if supernatural forces are bringing them together. Mr Rochester is aware of this. The next day, he says that that when he met her, he thought 'unaccountably of fairy tales' and suspected that she had 'bewitched' his horse. It seemed to him as if Jane was waiting for her 'people', the 'men in green' on the 'moonlight evening'. Jane mock-seriously says that they 'all forsook England a hundred years ago', showing her wit and sense of humour. The use of the supernatural therefore illustrates that psychologically, they are a good match for each other.

Jane appears to bewitch Mr Rochester. She observes him with Blanche, stating 'I saw he was going to marry her' because 'her rank and connections suited him'; however, Blanche 'could not charm him' like Jane can. Jane can see that Blanche and Mr Rochester are unsuited to each other, and Jane's ability to 'charm' him, highlights the difference between the two women. The verb 'charm' suggests magic and spells, again elevating her love for Mr Rochester above the ordinary. This is also supported by the use of italics for emphasis. The idea of an intense connection is developed when she states 'I have something in my brain and heart, in my blood and nerves, that assimilates me mentally to him'. They seem to possess a very close, spiritual bond.

The mood of the weather and in particular the appearance of the sky when Jane returns to Thornfield Hall after her visit to Gateshead strongly suggests magic and further develops the mythical element of the couple's relationship. The sky is compared to 'a fire lit, an altar burning behind its screen of marbled vapour, and out of apertures [shone] a golden redness'. The beautiful colours of the sunset create a feeling of the supernatural world descending to the ordinary world. The marriage imagery with the mention of the 'altar' also foreshadows the pending proposal. The red motif is a 'golden redness' connoting wealth: this implies that the meeting between the two after a month apart is a moment to be treasured and valued.

The fact that they are both involved in supernatural imagery develops the idea that they are spiritual equals. There are many examples of this in the novel; for example, upon Jane's return to Thornfield Hall, Mr Rochester asks if she can give him 'a charm' to make 'handsome'. Jane, demonstrating her wit, says that this 'would be past the power of magic' but adds 'A loving eye is all the charm needed'. It is obvious that they are flirting, and their spiritual connection is evident when she says that Mr Rochester 'had sometimes read my unspoken thoughts'. This reference to a psychic connection develops the idea that their love transcends the ordinary and foreshadows their psychic connection at the end of the Moor House chapters. It makes their love for each other extraordinary, contributing towards the eerie mood of the novel.

Finally, Mr Rochester's 'fairy' imagery to describe Jane could suggest impossible desires. In chapter 24, he tells Adèle that Jane is a 'fairy' from 'Elf-land', whose errand /is to make him 'happy'. He wants to go to Europe after their marriage and be 'healed and cleansed, with a very angel as my comforter'. Comparing Jane to an angel and a fairy suggests that he is hoping she will magically cleanse his soul of his past sins. In the Christian context of the early nineteenth century, this is quite a blasphemous hope, and a contemporary reader would have been shocked to read that, in the view of Mr Rochester, Jane, like God, was capable of cleansing people's sins.

Gothic Imagery

The gothic was a style of writing popular in late eighteenth-century England and was designed to thrill readers with accounts of villainy, murder, and the supernatural. The gothic employs dark and picturesque scenery, startling and melodramatic narrative devices, and an overall atmosphere of exoticism, mystery, and dread.

In 'Jane Eyre', Brontë employs a great deal of gothic imagery; we see the influences of the gothic with our first impression of Thornfield. The late, unfriendly servant drives Jane to Thornfield Hall through the 'misty' night. She hears the 'tolling' bell as they pass the church, and the entrance gates of Thornfield Hall 'clash' behind them. The 'dark' building is lit by 'candlelight'. Not only are these wonderfully atmospheric words, but they also foreshadow elements of Jane's life. The mist foreshadows her future inability to see her situation clearly as secrets will be hidden from her; bells usually toll at funerals, so the 'tolling' church bell could foreshadow the death of her hopes and expectations as well as the later death of Bertha Rochester; the 'clash' of the gates behind her might symbolise Bertha's imprisonment and Jane's future concerns about losing her identity in marriage; the 'dark' building could represent hidden secrets; and 'candlelight' has associations with Bertha's future attempts to burn down Thornfield, but might also remind the reader that, at Thornfield, Jane's passion and love for Mr Rochester will burn brightly. The gothic imagery therefore sets the scene and develops the idea of the supernatural controlling events.

Ancient and isolated places are one feature of gothic literature, and we see this in chapter 15 with the description of Thornfield Hall: 'its antiquity, its retirement, its old crow-trees and thorn-trees, its grey façade, and lines of dark windows reflecting that metal welkin' (sky). It is only because the Hall is isolated that Mr Rochester is able to hide his wife. The reference to 'crow-trees' remind us of crows, which symbolise death and misfortune. The 'thorn-trees' link to the name of the Hall and the fact that Jane will have many problems—she will metaphorically be walking through a field of thorns. The hard, dark colours of the Hall reflect the sky: we cannot see into the Hall. This imagery combines to create a tone of mystery, coldness and secrets.

When Jane arrives at Thornfield, we have the mystery of the absent master and the strange laughter. Another mystery is introduced in chapter 20 when Mr Rochester leads Jane through the 'dark, low corridor of the fateful third storey', and he takes her to one of its 'mystic cells' in the 'night' where she has the 'pale and bloody spectacle' of Mr Mason to tend. There is clearly a secret that Mr Rochester wishes to conceal from Jane when he orders Jane and Mason not to speak to each other.

Supernatural creatures are part of the gothic genre and, when Mr Mason tells Mr Rochester 'she worried me like a tigress' and 'she sucked the blood: she said she'd drain my heart', there is a strong reference to that most gothic of creatures—the vampire. Jane, like the reader, knows nothing of this mysterious 'she'. Later, she uses this imagery to describe Bertha Rochester as a 'Vampyre' when she tears Jane's wedding veil in half. Although Bertha is of course human, the secret and supernatural imagery develop suspense within the novel.

In gothic literature, references to the devil further amplify the horror...The terrible secrets of Thornfield Hall and the temptation of Jane into immorality imply the existence of Satan, or the devil. Jane thinks that the 'murderess' Grace Poole is 'a mocking demon' and 'a carrion-seeking bird of prey'; both are images associated with the devil, conjuring up thoughts of being toyed with by an evil being that is interested in dead flesh. She wonders how Mr Mason became involved in 'the web of horror'. This idea of 'horror' and being trapped in a 'web' like a fly, powerless to escape, is elaborated on when Jane imagines Judas threatening to reveal 'Satan'. In fact, the work of the devil will be revealed when we learn that Mr Rochester is concealing his wife and he subsequently tempts Jane to become his mistress.

The Imaginary Supernatural

There are references to the supernatural that can be easily explained but are of symbolic significance. For example, Mr Rochester pretends to be a gypsy, there to tell 'fortunes', which is a reference to the supernatural. The gypsy's otherness is emphasised when the footman describes 'her' as a 'shockingly ugly old creature' who is 'almost as black as a crock'. The ugliness connotes wickedness, and the dark imagery suggests a connection with the devil, hinting at Mr Rochester's promiscuous past and his future bigamous plans.

There is a moment when Mr Rochester disguised as a gypsy is like a witch, exerting a supernatural influence over Jane and casting a spell over her with words. She says that the gypsy's 'strange talk, voice, manner, had by this time wrapped me in a kind of dream'. She 'wondered what unseen spirit had been sitting for weeks by my heart watching its workings and taking record of every pulse'. It is at this point that the reader learns that Mr Rochester has been watching Jane as closely as she has been watching him. The reader also learns that, if he has a special skill, it is his ability to look into women's hearts (hence his comment that Blanche loves 'at least his purse'). Before Mr Rochester reveals his identity to Jane, he becomes more direct with her, hinting at his 'plans' and saying 'I think I rave in a kind of exquisite delirium'. Jane shares this moment: 'Had I been dreaming? Did I dream still?' Again, we have the suggestion of them meeting on a supernatural level, which moves their relationship beyond the ordinary limitations of human boundaries. Therefore, even though Mr Rochester is not a real gypsy, the gypsy disguise is significant in a number of ways.

Dreams

Jane's dreams, which are usually prophetic, are a further link to the supernatural theme. In chapter 15, she dreams of being 'tossed on a buoyant but unquiet sea, where billows of trouble rolled under surges of joy, but she is not able to reach the 'sweet hills'. The imagery suggests uncontrollable passion and suggests Jane's repressed desire for Mr Rochester. Her dream also foreshadows that she will experience turbulent times before she finally settles down with him, symbolised by the 'sweet hills'.

Dreams are also part of the supernatural theme; they are used as a device to prophesy death. In chapter 21, a week before the arrival of Robert Leaven (Mrs Reed's coachman), Jane dreams of a 'phantom-infant'. She comments that 'to dream of children was a sure sign of trouble, either to one's self or one's kin'. In this case, Leaven brings news that the shock of her cousin John Reed's suicide has resulted in Mrs Reed having a stroke and being on her deathbed. Here it is clear that Jane's dreams are prophetic, tying the novel more tightly to the supernatural.

This idea is further developed in chapter 22 with a dream that prophesies Jane's departure from Thornfield. She dreams of Blanche 'closing the gates of Thornfield' and 'pointing me out another road' while Mr Rochester is 'smiling sardonically'. The dream not only reveals Jane's insecurities about their pending marriage but also acts as a foreshadowing device.

Jane has two dreams the night before her wedding, both of which are significant and do not promise well for her marriage. In the first, she is following an 'unknown road', foreshadowing her departure from Thornfield to an uncertain future. She is 'burdened' with a 'little child', whom she associates with death, perhaps foreshadowing the death of Bertha Rochester, who is a burden to her husband. The child 'wailed piteously', which might symbolise bad prospects for their marriage. In this first dream, Jane 'strained' to 'overtake' Mr Rochester but, she tells him, her 'movements were fettered, and my voice still died away inarticulate; while you, I felt, withdrew farther and farther every moment.' This foreshadows the end of the Moor House chapters when they have a psychic connection in which Mr Rochester calls Jane's name, and his voice dies away.

In her second dream, Jane sees the 'dreary ruin' of Thornfield Hall and separation from Mr Rochester. This dream proves to be prophetic when Bertha Rochester burns down the Hall. Once more, there is the 'unknown little child', who clung around her neck and 'almost strangled' her. The child might also symbolise Jane's fears about not being able to create an independent role for herself within the marriage. (This would link to the 'doll' imagery in the previous chapter when Mr Rochester tried to buy Jane silk dresses.) Jane is used to earning her own money (however little) as a governess, and this dream might reflect Jane's anxieties about losing her independence when she becomes Mr Rochester's wife.

Finally, as we have seen in the *Structural Importance* subheading in this section, Jane is prompted to leave Thornfield Hall by her mother in a dream warning her to 'flee temptation'.

Motif of Ignis fatuus

Ignis fatuus is the Latin phrase for a will-o'-the-wisp, a phosphorescent light that hovers or floats at night, usually over marshy ground. This is a recurring motif within the novel and is a metaphor for a person or thing that is impossible to reach or catch. In chapter 16, Jane uses the idea of an *ignis fatuus* to describe her apparently impossible love for Mr Rochester, saying that it will lead her to 'the miry wilds whence there is no extrication'. This foreshadows her journey into the wilderness of the moors, which leads her to Moor House.

There is more foreshadowing in chapter 22 when Jane returns to Thornfield Hall after Gateshead. Mr Rochester jokes about Jane being an 'elf' and wonders if he dares to touch her, commenting 'I'd as soon offer to take hold of a blue *ignis fatuus* light in a marsh'. His comment foreshadows that he will not be able to keep hold of her, as she will leave Thornfield after their wedding day.

The *ignis fatuus* motif continues in chapter 27 when Mr Rochester explains that, after his disastrous marriage, he 'transformed' himself into a 'will-o'-the-wisp and travelled the continent'. This is another example of a supernatural connection that he and Jane share: Jane herself will become a will-o'-the-wisp when she leaves at the end of the chapter.

Finally, when she is on the moors, Jane sees candlelight in the window of the Rivers' house and at first believes it to be an *ignis fatuus*. The image becomes Christian, as the light leads her to Moor House and to God, symbolising hope for the future.

Theme and Context: Religion

Mr Brocklehurst

Religion is an important theme in the novel; Mr Brocklehurst symbolises Jane's aversion to some aspects of organised religion.

When Jane first meets Mr Brocklehurst in chapter 4, her description of him as 'a black pillar' strips Mr Brocklehurst of his humanity: like a 'pillar', he is hard and inflexible. In addition, his 'grim face' is 'like a carved mask', which adds to the impression of a cold man with no compassion. This creates a sense of unease because we wonder what the mask is hiding. It also foreshadows what we later learn of his hypocrisy, which is hidden behind a mask of Christianity. Jane exclaims, 'what a great nose! and what a mouth! and what large prominent teeth!', reminding the reader of the story of 'Little Red Riding Hood'. It is implied that Mr Brocklehurst is the big bad wolf; his character contrasts with the warmth and passion of Jane, his victim. The description of Mr Brocklehurst in his dark clothes is ironic for a so-called man of God. The reader is aware that—unlike the ballad sung by Bessie in chapter 3, which encourages an orphan to look to heaven for comfort—no comfort will be provided by Mr Brocklehurst.

In chapter 6, we learn more about Mr Brocklehurst's hypocrisy when he quotes the Bible to justify his opinions. For example, he criticises Mrs Temple for supplying lunch to replace the children's inedible breakfast of burnt porridge and he says 'If ye suffer hunger or thirst for My sake, happy are ye'. However, his own children are warm and well-fed. We therefore see his cruelty when he attempts to reduce the children to the lowest level of degradation to which it is possible.

The full extent of his hypocrisy can be seen when, after insisting that the pupils must not become used to 'habits of luxury and indulgence', he orders Miss Temple to have a girl's naturally curly hair 'cut off entirely'. He then says that the remaining girls' 'top-knots must be cut off'. In contrast, we see that his daughters have 'a profusion of light tresses, elaborately curled' while Mrs Brocklehurst is wearing 'a false front of French curls.' Not only does this hypocrisy encourage the reader to judge Mr Brocklehurst's commitment to his religion, but it leads the reader to question where the money to clothe his wife and daughters has come from. It is implied (but never explicitly stated) that Mr Brocklehurst is embezzling funds that are allocated to the welfare of the pupils.

St. John Rivers

We first meet St. John when he, like a shepherd helping a wandering sheep, takes the destitute Jane into his house. On his doorstep, she gives herself up to the will of God: 'I believe in God. Let me try to wait His will in silence.' The reader is led to feel that God is working through St. John in answer to Jane's prayers. Although the pastor is associated with ice and snow imagery (see *Theme and Context: Passion versus Restraint*), the imagery is white, symbolising his goodness. Brontë emphasises this when Jane and Diana comment that he is a 'good man'. St John Rivers' colour associations contrast with the black imagery of Mr Brocklehurst, who serves as a foil.

While Mr Brocklehurst uses religion to support his hypocritical views, St. John is 'zealous' and 'blameless in his life and habits'; however, he is not happy: 'he yet did not appear to enjoy that mental serenity, that inward content, which should be the reward of every sincere Christian and practical philanthropist'. He deals with his internal conflict through his desire to do missionary work. In chapter 34, he uses robust masculine imagery to describe God as 'my king, my lawgiver, my captain'. The repetition of 'my' and the triplet of nouns together build his passion for God, a passion which contrasts directly with his self-restraint in worldly relationships. He develops war imagery when proposing to Jane, wanting her to 'enlist' under the Christian 'banner'. We see his influence on Jane when she employs the same imagery, refusing his offer of marriage but volunteering to accompany him as 'comrade' or 'fellow-soldier'. St. John wants her to 'wrench' her 'heart' from humanity and 'fix' it on upon God. The verb 'wrench' is another violent word that demonstrates St. John's severity and determination to focus on God. St. John therefore rejects earthly concerns to serve God while—in direct contrast—the hypocritical Mr Brocklehurst uses God to justify his actions.

Helen Burns

Helen Burns, who is far more spiritual and less worldly than Mr Brocklehurst, also serves as his foil. She illustrates the Christian attitudes of compassion and forgiveness that are lacking in Mr Brocklehurst. Instead of quoting the scriptures as Mr Brocklehurst does to justify his opinions, she quotes the New Testament to comfort Jane, advising her to 'Love your enemies; bless them that curse you; do good to them that hate you and despitefully use you'. Helen preaches the Christian doctrine of endurance and, unlike the hypocritical Mr Brocklehurst, leads by example.

When Helen, Mrs Temple and Jane eat seed cake and talk, Helen's goodness and spirituality appear to come straight from God: 'her soul sat on her lips, and language flowed, from what source I cannot tell.' The personification of her soul suggests her innate goodness and sincerity, which again contrasts with Mr Brocklehurst. It is almost as if, with her 'pure, full, fervid eloquence', she is too good for this world. It is significant that her soul is on her lips: it is not within her body. This implies that it will soon take flight to heaven when she passes on.

There is light imagery associated with Helen, which contrasts with the dark imagery that we have seen with Mr Brocklehurst. The name Helen is Greek for 'torch' and this fits with her surname 'Burns'. Jane sees that Helen burns with the light of God when she is forced by Mr Brocklehurst to stand on a stool; a 'ray' of 'strange light' in Helen's eyes comforts Jane. This Christ-like imagery creates 'an extraordinary sensation' in Jane. Helen burns brightly while she lives and then, like Maria and Elizabeth Brontë, dies young.

Helen also serves as a foil to Jane, as the former burns with a desire for the afterlife while the latter focuses on the worldly. Helen tells Jane that 'Life appears to me too short to be spent in nursing animosity or registering wrongs'; this is ironic because life for her will be short. Conversely, she might be aware that she is going to die. Helen tells Jane: 'you think too much of the love of human beings; you are too impulsive, too vehement', implying that she should be more concerned with the love of God. Her refusal to focus on the real world therefore contrasts with Jane's attitude. Like St. John, Helen's thoughts are on God, but she shows more compassion towards others than he does.

Another contrast between the girls can be seen when Helen is on her deathbed. She says: 'I believe; I have faith: I am going to God', and Jane replies 'Where is God? What is God?'. Jane cannot fully put her trust in God: for Jane, heaven is beauty on earth, hence the detailed description at the start of chapter 9 of Lowood in the spring, which is full of new life and hope ('great elm, ash, and oak skeletons were restored to majestic life').

Later in the novel, we read about the 'grey marble tablet' that marks Helen's grave, and we assume that Jane has paid for it. The Latin inscription 'Resurgam' means 'I will rise again' and illustrates Helen's faith that she will one day rise again to meet her maker. If we move from the spiritual to the earthly, it might also symbolise Jane's ability to rise again after her past, present and future troubles.

Sin, Divine Retribution, Forgiveness and Redemption

In parts of the novel, Jane suggests that God directly intervenes in our lives. We have already been introduced to the theme of divine retribution after Mr Rochester's marriage proposal. The subsequent storm and the chestnut tree being struck in half by lightning suggest the wrath of God (see *Language: Pathetic Fallacy*).

At the end of chapter 24, Jane states that she loves Mr Rochester more than she loves God: 'My future husband was becoming to me my whole world; and more than the world: almost my hope of heaven'. Christian readers would interpret this comment as blasphemous, and argue that Jane's hardships in chapter 28 are divine retribution for her earlier placement of Mr Rochester before God.

Brontë was influenced by the Romantic movement, which placed great importance on the powerful emotional experience generated by the contemplation of nature. When Jane is on the moors in chapter 28, she sees God in nature as 'benign and good' like a 'mother'. Through the beauty of nature, she feels God's 'presence most when His works are on the grandest scale spread before us; and it is in the unclouded night-sky, where His worlds wheel their silent course, that we read clearest His infinitude, His omnipotence, His omnipresence'. Jane sees Heaven on earth through the natural world, and she finds consolation in this thought.

Her arrival at Moor House marks the beginning of the last part of Jane's journey of self-discovery. The loss of her parcel (containing 'some linen, a locket, a ring') in the coach symbolises that she must shed all connections to the past to rebuild herself and gain forgiveness from God. There is further Christian imagery of rebirth in chapter 29, when Jane is ill at Moor House for 'about three days and nights ', which reminds us of the length of time between the crucifixion and resurrection of Christ. This symbolises Jane being metaphorically reborn into a new family.

As we have seen, God appears to answer Jane's prayers before St. John takes her in and then once again after she appeals to Him for guidance when St. John is proposing. After her shared psychic experience with Mr Rochester, she says 'I prayed in my way—a different way to St. John's, but effective in its own fashion. I seemed to penetrate very near a Mighty Spirit; and my soul rushed out in gratitude at His feet'. Now that she is 'at his feet', we have the visual metaphor of her being humbled. There is a sense of a personal connection with God and the feeling that she has been forgiven for her sins.

The Christian belief of repenting, paying penance and being forgiven can also be seen in chapter 37. Mr Rochester realises that had Jane become his mistress, he would have 'sullied' her. He admits that, after she left, he 'cursed' and 'defied' God, who punished him through 'Divine justice'. He says he started to feel 'remorse, repentance; the wish for reconcilement' with God and he 'began sometimes to pray'. It is during one of his prayers that he asked God in 'anguish and humility' if he could 'taste bliss and peace once more'. It was at this point that he shouted Jane's name. In the same way that God appeared to be answering Jane's prayers in chapter 35, God seems to be answering Mr Rochester's prayers (Mr Rochester says 'In spirit, I believe we must have met'). Now that he has been 'humbled', Mr Rochester, like Jane, is ready to find redemption through religion.

Theme and Context: The Family/Home

Although Jane is living with relations at Gateshead, she is a poor dependent, made to feel inferior and does not have the love or respect of her family. Her cousin John Reed says: 'you ought to beg, and not to live here with gentleman's children like us'. Isolated and alienated, Jane is not an accepted member of the family; John and his sisters have absorbed Mrs Reed's attitude and poverty of spirit.

Moreover, Mrs Reed does not fulfil her duty of care to Jane: she punishes Jane unfairly and allows bullying; she engages the apothecary Mr Lloyd to treat Jane rather than the more expensive and better trained family doctor; furthermore, she sends the young Jane unaccompanied to the charity school Lowood. This is a callous attitude towards a dependent, especially when Mrs Reed had promised her husband to raise Jane as her own. Finally, Mrs Reed, who should be protecting Jane, provides Mr Brocklehurst with ammunition for future bullying by declaring that she is a liar. All of these examples emphasise Mrs Reed's lack of Christian charity.

Before Jane leaves Gateshead, she passionately declares to Mrs Reed: 'I am glad you are no relation of mine: I will never call you aunt again as long as I live'. In rejecting Mrs Reed, we see Jane freeing herself emotionally. We realise that merely having relatives in a house, does not make a house a home. The theme of home being a place of like-minded people who share love is developed in chapter 22 when Jane tells Mr Rochester 'wherever you are is my home—my only home'. We therefore see that, for Jane, home is to do with people rather than a place.

Miss Temple is a better mother figure to Jane, in distinct contrast to Mrs Reed. Miss Temple is aptly named: she embodies goodness, and the pupils metaphorically worship her. A good Christian, she nurtures the hungry children, showing compassion and financial generosity when she orders lunch after the inedible porridge. Her first name is Maria which invokes the name of Jesus' mother (and possibly Brontë's mother), suggesting that Brontë is deliberately depicting Miss Temple as a maternal figure. In Victorian times, people believed that a person's appearance reflected their personality— Miss Temple is 'tall, fair, and shapely', has 'refined features; a complexion, if pale, clear; and a stately air and carriage'. All of these words have positive connotations of nobility and innate goodness. We see that a substitute, unrelated mother figure can be better at nurturing than the close relative Mrs Reed, who raised Jane from a baby.

Jane's relationships with her substitute family (Helen Burns becomes a sister substitute) are so important to her that they enable her to bear the cruelties of Lowood: she declares 'I would not now have exchanged Lowood with all its privations, for Gateshead and its daily luxuries'. As far as Jane is concerned, not only is home a place where one is accepted by others, but it has the benefits of developing herself as a person.

Jane's attitude towards home is rationalised when she visits the Reeds at Gateshead. In chapter 21, she says 'I still felt as a wanderer on the face of the earth; but I experienced firmer trust in myself and my own powers, and less withering dread of oppression'. She emphasises that, as a 'wanderer', she does not feel that she is returning home, but her self-confidence has improved since she was a child. The concept of home is therefore used to illustrate Jane's development.

We also see a contrast between the faults of the Reed siblings and Jane's exemplary behaviour; this is Brontë's way of encouraging the reader to witness how poor behaviour is the result of an indulged upbringing. The Reed sisters are caricatures of each other. Eliza is outwardly religious, symbolised by her 'crucifix' and desire to become a nun. Her poor, ungenerous inner spirit, however, is shown by the fact that she is 'thin', she has an unhealthy 'sallow face and severe' expression, and her routine is unproductive: Jane finds no 'result of her diligence'. She is 'bitter' and judgemental and, like Mr Brocklehurst, she lacks compassion. She looks at her mother 'calmly' when she dies and does not even cry. Perhaps she does not weep because she dislikes her mother; or she might lack the capacity to express grief because she was brought up by an emotionally inhibited mother. Brontë's negative depiction of Eliza illustrates that, like Mr Brocklehurst, we should not automatically assume that all religious people are good people.

Georgiana contrasts with Eliza, as she lacks judgement and is full of feeling. She overindulges her body, being 'very plump'. With her 'languishing blue eyes, and ringleted yellow hair', she is much prettier than her sister. Her dress 'looked as stylish as the other's [Eliza's] looked puritanical'. She only appears, however, to be interested in 'herself, her loves, and woes'. Like Eliza, she is not affected by 'her mother's illness, or her brother's death, or the present gloomy state of the family prospects'. Both Georgiana and Eliza are extremes: Georgiana is too full of feeling while Eliza is too judgemental. They contrast with Jane, who has a better balance of feelings and judgement. Perhaps Brontë is suggesting that we should judge attractive people by their personal qualities rather than being taken in by their looks.

The reader learns more of the consequences of poor parenting with the overindulged John Reed, who 'ruined his health and his estate amongst the worst men and the worst women'. Mr Rochester calls him the 'one of the veriest rascals' with his 'debts' and 'suicide'. By way of contrast, Jane's exemplary behaviour is the result of having a sound education and positive role models at Lowood.

From a religious point of view, the dying Mrs Reed should be forgiving others their sins because in the afterlife, she hopes to be forgiven for her own sins. Instead, as Jane says, 'living, she had ever hated me—dying, she must hate me still'. Mrs Reed manages to 'ease' her 'mind' by giving Jane the letter from John Eyre and admitting that she had told him Jane was dead. She also says that she wished Jane 'had died' at Lowood. Covering up Jane's existence and wishing her dead are both shocking indictments of Mrs Reed's character. She refuses to be 'reconciled' with Jane who, like a good Christian, gives her in return 'full and free forgiveness'. Or so she claims (see *Form and Genre: Decision 1*. The older Jane addresses the dead Mrs Reed, saying 'I ought to forgive you', implying that she has not).

We never meet John Eyre, but his character serves as an important plot device: in response to his letter, Jane writes to him to announce her marriage and thus begins a chain of events. John Eyre will immediately know about the 'impediment' and persuade

Mr Mason to return to Thornfield Hall with a lawyer to stop the wedding. Finally, John Eyre will leave all his money to Jane, giving her the independence that she needs. Earlier in the novel, Bessie comments that he is a 'gentleman'. Through hard work, he makes his fortune, which he does not squander like John Reed. He is generous in leaving his money to Jane, whom he has never met. He is a more caring member of Jane's family than the Reeds.

Furthermore, we see that although Jane feels immediately at home in Moor House, others do not initially view her in this light. Diana, upon finding Jane in the kitchen, says 'you are a visitor, and must go into the parlour'. By treating her in this way, Diana is reminding Jane of her status and perhaps is subtly telling her that she should not be wandering around the house as if it were her home.

The Rivers sisters serve as contrasts to the Reed sisters, heightening the differences between both pairs of female siblings. When Jane learns that the Reeds are her cousins, she takes 'delicious pleasure' in having a loving family, declaring 'I never had a home, I never had brothers or sisters; I must and will have them now'. The repetition of 'I never' coupled with the auxiliary verbs 'must' and 'will' serve to emphasise her delight in the fact that she is related to like-minded people. This reminds the reader of what was absent from her relationship with her Reed cousins.

Traditionally, the wealth of upper-class families was inherited by the oldest son to keep the family estate intact; therefore, Mr Rochester as a younger son had to marry a rich heiress. Although Jane is a female, she defies the tradition of keeping her inheritance to herself when she shares it with her cousins. St. John finds this difficult to understand: 'it is contrary to all custom'. Jane, who 'never had a home', prioritises family and rejects 'society' in favour of her family. To Jane, a loving family is more important than money. With the money equally shared, Diana and Mary will be restored to their position in society, and Jane will be able to heal the old divisions between the Rivers' father and John Eyre.

Theme and Context: Attitudes to Foreigners

The British Empire

In Victorian times, the British Empire was expanding and creating opportunities for individuals such as John Eyre to make their fortunes. Many contemporary views about Britain's colonies, especially India and the West Indies, are reflected in the novel. The novel also explores Victorian attitudes towards anyone who is not English.

Cecil Rhodes, a British businessman, mining magnate and the Prime Minister of the Cape Colony (from 1890 to 1896) said: 'Remember that you are an Englishman, and have consequently won first prize in the lottery of life'. Not only did the Victorians have a strong sense of their own place in the social hierarchy, but they liked to maintain a hierarchy between themselves and people from other countries.

Attitudes to the French

Blanche calls Adèle a 'little puppet', which strips her of her identity and reduces her to the level of a pretty doll, novelty entertainment for the guests. In addition, the French dialogue in the Thornfield chapters emphasises Adèle's otherness. For example, she cheerfully exclaims 'Ma boîte! ma boîte!' and Mr Rochester comments that she is a 'genuine daughter of Paris', only being interested in clothes and pretty objects.

Through Adèle, we learn more about English attitudes to French women. Adèle sings 'a song from some opera' about a woman whose lover has left her, and Jane feels that the 'subject seemed strangely chosen for an infant singer'. This hints at the foreign mother's promiscuity and emphasises the importance of Jane's role in teaching Adèle moral English ways. At the end of the novel, we learn that Adèle's 'sound English education' has 'corrected in a great measure her French defects'. The older Adèle now conforms to English standards of behaviour. There is a sense of satisfaction that a solid English education has eliminated any faults such as immorality and materialism (valuing possessions more than spiritual values) that Adèle might have inherited from her mother.

The Victorian idea of the continent being a corrupt place where English people go to indulge in immoral behaviour is developed in chapter 29. Jane asks herself if it might be 'better' to 'have surrendered to temptation' and to be 'living in France' as 'Mr. Rochester's mistress'. This contrasts with the idea of the morally correct life that Jane at this point in the novel is experiencing as 'a village-schoolmistress, free and honest', living 'in the healthy heart of England'.

It is implied that Céline is a manipulative foreign Frenchwoman who took advantage of Mr Rochester by charming the 'English gold' out of his 'British breeches' (chapter 14). This emphasis on 'English' and 'British' depicts him as a noble victim gulled by an unscrupulous foreign gold-digger, and thus contemporary readers might feel sympathy towards him. A modern and less prejudiced reader is not as likely to be sympathetic, bearing in mind that he was a married man at the time of his affair. Nevertheless, his subsequent dislike of 'artificial' materialism in the sense of superficial values might explain his growing attraction to Jane, who is an obvious contrast to Céline Varens in matters of money and possessions.

Attitudes to the Inhabitants of the West Indies

In the novel, we learn that Victorians perceived dark skin to be undesirable, associated as it was with foreigners. Jane notes in chapter 18 that Mr Mason is 'not precisely foreign, but still not altogether English'. His mother is a Creole (of mixed European and black descent); unaware of this, Jane notes his 'singularly sallow' complexion, and his face 'failed to please'. His 'odd look' or appearance 'repelled' Jane 'exceedingly'. Jane's prejudice would probably pass unchallenged by readers at the time; a modern reader is unlikely to accept Jane's views.

Bertha Rochester, Mr Mason's sister, is also half Creole. When Jane describes Bertha as 'savage', 'blackened', with 'swelled and dark' lips and 'black eyebrows', she is describing a woman of mixed race and turning her (as if she were a 'Vampyre') into a creature of supernatural horror. This takes the fear and mistrust of foreigners to an extreme.

Victorian prejudice against foreigners was particularly pointed if they were women. We learn that Bertha's 'mother, the Creole, was both a madwoman and a drunkard'. Bertha inherits her 'infamous' behaviour from her mother, and we are aware that Adèle inherits her vanity and love for material possessions from her mother. In the patriarchal English society of the time, bad blood appears to be more readily inherited from foreign women.

Belief in Christian Superiority

In chapter 24, we see another example of English superiority when Jane limits Mr Rochester's expenditure on new clothes and jewellery. Her references to a 'Grand Turk's' harem ('seraglio') and its associations of 'slave purchases' and 'tons of flesh' reflect her reluctance to become his legal possession. She defends her independence, saying that she will become 'a missionary to preach liberty to them that are enslaved— your harem inmates amongst the rest' and she will 'stir up mutiny'. Here, we see that the idea of an Englishwoman rescuing Turkish women and imposing her Christian religion on them is acceptable. This parallels the missionary plans of St. John in the Moor House chapters.

Not only was it acceptable to impose one's own beliefs on others, but the Victorians believed they had an obligation to do so. In chapter 31, St. John states that 'God had an errand' for him as a 'missionary'. This illustrates contemporary attitudes of English and Christian superiority. In India, we learn that St. John Rivers, 'firm, faithful, and devoted, full of energy, and zeal, and truth' continues to work hard 'for his race'. The triplets of adjectives and nouns emphasise his fervour and his view that the population of India is inferior. Converting its inhabitants is 'painful' but he 'hews down like a giant the prejudices of creed and caste'. Note his lack of respect for the views of the indigenous population of India: the focus is on their prejudices and his correct judgement. This develops the idea of St. John fighting God's war.

Finally, we have English prejudice with the assumption that living in India will kill Jane. After St. John proposes, Jane states 'if I go to India, I go to premature death'. She provides no evidence to support this view, but it foreshadows St. John's early death, thereby confirming contemporary beliefs.

Theme and Context: Education

The Lowood School chapters depict life in a charitable school in the early 19th century. Through the eyes of Jane, we are introduced to its routines. Some of the characters and experiences (see *Author* and *Theme and Context: Religion*) are based on real people and events.

Some Victorians believed that it was against nature for women to study because it made them ill. Instead, middle- and upper-class women were often required to play an ornamental role hence the value that society placed on their looks. Girls were raised to marry and have children; consequently, their education was more restricted than that of boys, and women were unable to pursue the career options open to men. The first university in the UK to award degrees to women was the University of London in 1878, twenty-four years after the death of Brontë.

Part of a 'good English education' for middle- and upper-class women included the study of history, geography and literature. This would provide them with interesting but non-controversial subjects to talk about. As long as a girl was pretty and accomplished enough to attract a husband and entertain his guests, that was deemed sufficient.

Opportunities for middle-class women to work in respectable jobs were limited in Victorian times, so education was the only means by which Jane could develop the skills and knowledge to establish an independent place for herself in society. She received an 'excellent education' at Lowood School, and this qualified her to become a governess. Nevertheless, the older Jane comments that, when she advertised her 'good English education, together with French, Drawing, and Music', this is now regarded as a 'narrow catalogue of accomplishments'. 'Accomplishments' included playing the piano, singing, dancing and flower-arranging. If a woman could speak another language, she would be more likely to find employment as a governess but, like Brontë, many women found this an unappealing way to make a living. Note that the moment the Rivers sisters have an independent income, they choose to stop working as governesses.

Comments from other characters emphasise Jane's knowledge, skills and experience. For example, when Bessie visits Jane, she says 'The Miss Reeds could not play as well!' Bessie therefore provides the reader with external validation of Jane's attainment—something about which the older Jane would not boast. It is also ironic that the Reeds, with the money to lavish on education, have not made the most of their advantages. Jane's educational achievements therefore encourage the reader to regard her as superior to her upper-class cousins.

The reader receives independent confirmation of Jane's ability as a teacher when Mr Rochester praises her for Adèle's progress: 'in a short time she has made much improvement'. Dialogue is an effective way to convey this message, as modesty probably stops the older Jane from directly telling us that she is a good teacher.

Education is part of Jane's healing when she exchanges knowledge and skills with her Rivers cousins. She states 'Diana offered to teach me German. I liked to learn of her', reminding the reader of Jane's time as a student at Lowood. Diana is a role model, just like Miss Temple and Helen Burns, and we realise once again that Jane finds solace in education and educated women.

In chapter 29, Jane is offered the position of 'mistress' of a girls' charity school in Morton. Education offers a 'humble' yet 'sheltered' and 'safe asylum', so provides the means for Jane to retreat from the world and continue the healing process. The adjective 'humble', however, suggests that she is keenly aware of the contrast between this and her previous position.

Moreover, in chapter 31, Jane reminds herself that she 'must not forget that these coarsely-clad little peasants are of flesh and blood as good as the scions of gentlest genealogy; and that the germs of native excellence, refinement, intelligence, kind feeling, are as likely to exist in their hearts as in those of the best-born'. Jane is reminding herself that her village school children have just as much potential as better born children. This is ironic because we have seen lots of examples of poor behaviour with the Reeds and Blanche Ingram, yet Jane still states that 'refinement, intelligence' and 'kind feeling' are attributes of the upper classes.

Nevertheless, Jane admits that she feels 'degraded' by her position as school mistress. She has taken a step that 'sank' instead of 'raising' her 'in the scale of social existence'. Her keen awareness of her drop in social status can be seen in the way she regards her pupils. It is ironic that Jane has been a beggar because she is now filled with 'disgust' at the 'ignorance' and 'coarseness', of her lower-class pupils (the 'little peasants'). In a telling contrast, it is significant that she described Adèle's personality in detail, even reporting her words, yet we learn nothing about her individual pupils in Morton, not even their names. This suggests a lack of interest in their individual identities because of their low social status.

Characters

Jane's character has been described in this guide in detail. The remaining main characters are summarised below.

Gateshead Characters

Mrs Reed

Mrs Reed is Jane's aunt by marriage (Mrs Reed's husband was brother to Jane's mother). She is cruel to Jane because her husband, Mr Reed, seemed to prefer Jane to his own children. A reed is a tall, grass-like plant that grows in marshes or water. Its height connotes Mrs Reed's social status, but marshland is unhealthy, symbolising how Mrs Reed creates a negative environment at Gateshead: she packs Jane off to a charity school at the age of ten; wishes that she had died of typhus at Lowood; lies to John Eyre by informing him that Jane is dead; and refuses to reconcile herself with her niece on her deathbed. Her character is important because we see that a high social class does not necessarily equate to exemplary behaviour. Mrs Reed's character is important, as the letter she eventually passes to Jane changes her life.

Mr Reed

Uncle Reed is Mrs Reed's late husband. When he was dying, he made Mrs Reed promise to treat Jane as one of her own children. Mrs Reed breaks this promise, and it is in the red-room that Jane believes she sees Uncle Reed's ghost returning to avenge itself on his wife.

John Reed

Mrs Reed has three children. John, Jane's cousin, is the only boy. As a child, he bullies Jane and throws a book at her. As an adult, he drinks, gambles, gets into debt and commits suicide. His first name is ironic because it means 'gracious'. Perhaps Brontë is suggesting that, had he been less indulged as a child, he might have matured into a much better person.

Eliza Reed

Eliza (she has the title of Miss Reed because she is the elder sister) is Jane's cousin and John's sister. She is hard and inflexible, showing no sadness when Mrs Reed dies. She joins a French convent and eventually becomes its Mother Superior.

Georgiana Reed

Beautiful, self-centred and vain, Georgiana is Jane's cousin and John's sister. As a child, she treated Jane cruelly, but she is more friendly as an adult. Georgiana and Eliza do not like each other because Eliza told their mother of Georgiana's plans to elope. After the death of Mrs Reed, Georgiana shows no grief and promptly marries a wealthy man.

Both Georgiana and Eliza's names aim to impress. They contrast greatly with plain Jane and the names of Diana and Mary Rivers.

Bessie Lee

Bessie works as a maid at Gateshead. Although she can be strict, she treats Jane kindly by telling her stories and singing songs. Bessie demonstrates the goodness at Gateshead; her character contrasts with the oppressive Mrs Reed and Mr Brocklehurst. Bessie marries the coachman, Robert Leaven.

Mr. Lloyd

Mr. Lloyd is a kind apothecary, who treats the servants and Jane. He suggests that Jane be sent to school where he hopes she will be happier. Miss Temple writes to ask him about the allegation, initiated by Mrs Reed, that Jane is a liar. Mr Lloyd confirms Jane's story and clears her name.

John Eyre

Although we never meet the wealthy wine merchant John Eyre, we associate him with Gateshead, Thornfield Hall and Moor House. We hear that he visits Gateshead in search of Jane when she is at Lowood School. He writes to Mrs Reed, announcing that he would like to adopt Jane, take her to Madeira and make her his heir. When Jane writes to him to announce her pending marriage to Mr Thornfield, he dispatches Mr Briggs to declare an impediment. This is for the best of motives, as he wants to protect Jane. Then he dies and leaves her 20,000 pounds, which she shares with her Rivers cousins. Years before, he had badly advised Mr Rivers, who subsequently lost a lot of money. This resulted in an argument and an estrangement between the two sides of the family. Consequently, John Eyre chose not to leave any money to the Rivers family. Like Jane, we associate him with travel.

Lowood School Characters

Mr Brocklehurst

Cruel and hypocritical, Mr Brocklehurst is the master of Lowood School. In direct contrast to his wife and daughters, he believes that the pupils of Lowood School should be humbled and semi-starved to encourage them to focus more on God. He uses religion to support his views and to control others. After the typhus epidemic and subsequent enquiry into conditions at the school, he loses management of Lowood.

Miss Temple

Maria Temple is a mother figure to Jane and the Lowood pupils. Her kindness in ordering lunch for the girls, who were unable to eat the burnt porridge, contrasts with Mr Brocklehurst's harshness. She is a positive female role model; under her influence, Jane learns to control her passions. When Miss Temple later marries a clergyman, Jane decides to leave Lowood School.

Helen Burns

Helen is Jane's good friend, and she dies of consumption in Jane's arms. Her genuinely religious character serves as a foil to Mr Brocklehurst. Helen also serves as a foil to Jane: unlike Jane, she tolerates and accepts harsh treatment from others. She is also consoled by thoughts of life after death, believing that God will punish or reward. Jane, on the other hand, prefers to think about life, love and happiness in this world rather than the next.

Miss Scatcherd

Miss Scatcherd is Miss Temple's opposite. The onomatopoeia of her name has connotations of scratching, scars and catching. Her name is therefore apt, as it creates the impression of malevolence. This is seen when she bullies and flogs Helen with a bunch of twigs.

Thornfield Hall Characters

Mr Rochester

The wealthy landowner Edward Rochester is master of Rochester Hall and Ferndean Manor. The first part of Edward means 'wealth' and the second part 'guard', so his name symbolises his position in society as a man with inherited wealth. It also reminds us that his problems are because he married the rich Bertha Rochester: this was because his father kept the Rochester family estate in one piece by leaving it all to Mr Rochester's elder brother. Mr Rochester guards Bertha by keeping her locked away.

There are both positive and negative sides to his character. The positive aspects are that he could have hidden Bertha in the unhealthy dampness of Ferndean to die a premature death, or he could have had her committed to a mental asylum; he tries to rescue her when she sets fire to Thornfield Hall; and, when there is no evidence that he is Adèle's father, he makes her his ward. On the negative side, he is an adulterer and has had a string of mistresses. He also conceals the existence of his wife and attempts bigamy.

As discussed earlier, Mr Rochester believes that he can be cleansed through Jane's love. After his failed bigamous marriage, his deliberate attempt to corrupt Jane results in her departure, demonstrating that morally she is superior to him.

In the eyes of God, he must be punished for his sins before he repents and can marry Jane, hence his injuries (divine punishment or retribution) when Thornfield Hall burns down. Jane also changes: she inherits money, gains a family and had been on the point of abandoning passion. She has grown in strength and, although she marries Mr Rochester as a spiritual equal with no secrets, his dependence on her alters the dynamics of the relationship.

Bertha Mason

When Mr Rochester married Bertha, a beautiful, wealthy woman of Creole descent, he was not aware of her promiscuity. Violent and mad, she embodies the uncontrolled passions of sexuality and anger. She is locked in a secret room and cared for by Grace Poole, but escapes when Grace becomes drunk. Bertha adds to the gothic elements of the novel, as Jane initially thinks that she is a 'ghost'. Bertha never speaks, perhaps symbolising the lack of rights that Victorian women had in their marriages. Her role is to be an impediment to Jane and Mr Rochester's marriage. Through her death, Mr Rochester can suffer, repent and atone for his sins before marrying Jane.

Bertha is a Germanic name that means 'bright' or 'famous'. We associate her with the brightness of the fires that she starts, and she becomes famous (or infamous) once her existence is discovered. According to Germanic legends, Bertha is the goddess of animals, and this might link to the animal imagery that Jane uses to describe her in her madness. Her maiden name Mason means 'stoneworker'. The name 'Rochester' looks like 'rock'—she, a mason, works many changes on his character.

Mrs Fairfax

Alice Fairfax, a distant relation by marriage, is Mr Rochester's housekeeper at Thornfield Hall. 'Alice' is derived from 'Adelaide', which means 'noble' and 'kind'. She warmly welcomes Jane to Thornfield, revealing that she has been lonely because she has to keep her distance from the lower-class servants. Jane's welcome from Mrs Fairfax is the first indication that she will come to think of Thornfield as her home. Mrs Fairfax tells Jane that Grace Poole is responsible for the strange laughter. She also warns Jane to keep Mr Rochester at a distance until they are married. Eventually, Mrs Fairfax is provided with a generous pension.

Grace Poole

Grace Poole is employed to look after Bertha Mason but, when she has drunk too much gin, her patient often escapes. Grace becomes the scapegoat for Bertha's mysterious laughter, and Jane is encouraged to believe that Grace set fire to Mr Rochester's bed curtains.

Adèle Varens

Adèle is the reason for Jane's employment at Thornfield Hall. She is the daughter of Céline Varens, a French opera-dancer, who was unfaithful to Mr Rochester. Mr Rochester brings Adèle to Thornfield Hall after her mother abandons her despite not believing that she is his daughter. As a child, she is vain and spoilt, but she matures into a 'pleasing and obliging companion'.

Mr Mason

Richard Mason is Bertha Rochester's brother. When he visits her at Thornfield Hall, she stabs and bites him. Jane's uncle, John Eyre, tells Mr Mason about her intended marriage and sends him to stop the wedding.

Mr Briggs

Mr Briggs is John Eyre's solicitor. Acting upon his instructions, Mr Briggs helps Mr Mason to prevent Jane's marriage. He also initiates a search for Jane after her uncle dies so that she can receive her inheritance.

Blanche Ingram

The beautiful and wealthy socialite Blanche Ingram is cruel to Jane; we learn a lot about how governesses were regarded in upper-class families from her comments. She is Jane's competitor for the love of Mr Rochester, but Blanche is only interested in his money.

Blanche is French for 'white', which is ironic, as white connotes goodness, which is not reflected in her character. While Jane prefers dark 'Quakerish' clothes (which symbolise her modesty and contrast with the clothes of the aristocrats), Blanche wears 'pure white clothes', which connote bridal gowns. This emphasises Jane's feelings that Blanche is a threat. However, the negative side to her personality is implied with her 'large and black' eyes and 'raven-black' hair. We know that the Victorians associated darkness with evil, so her eyes and hair colour hint at her black heart.

Blanche Ingram has a competitive attitude to marriage, which contrasts with that of Jane and Mr Rochester. In the drawing room at Thornfield Hall, she says 'I am resolved my husband shall not be a rival, but a foil to me… I shall exact an undivided homage'. In other words, in a marriage, partners should be different to each other: she does not want a husband to be as attractive as her because she wants all the attention. This view of marriage contrasts with the spiritual connection that Jane and Mr Rochester share. It also illustrates that Blanche and Mr Rochester are incompatible.

Moor House Characters

St. John Rivers

St. John is Jane's cousin (his mother was sister to brothers John Eyre and Jane's father). Not knowing that they are related, the young, handsome clergyman offers Jane shelter out of charity, finds work for her and asks her to marry him. He does not love Jane but feels that she would make a good missionary's wife. He is a zealous despot and serves as Mr Rochester's foil, suppressing his love for Rosamond Oliver and refusing to allow his feelings to rule him. We associate St. John with ice, snow and rock imagery, reflecting his cool, hard nature. In contrast, we associate Mr Rochester with passionate fire imagery.

St. John's final letter to Jane contains the words 'Come, Lord Jesus', which also end the novel. These words are from 'Revelation', one of five New Testament books written by St. John the Apostle, who was one of Jesus' twelve Apostles. The surname Rivers also connotes John the Baptist, who baptised Jesus. This combined religious imagery foreshadows his work as a missionary.

Moreover, a river is a flowing body of water that in literature symbolises a literal or metaphorical journey. St. John Rivers helps Jane by saving her from wandering the moors and putting her on the path of work. Although St. John does not love her, his proposals of marriage progress Jane's spiritual journey, as she learns that she needs mutual love to be happy. The psychic connection that she has with Mr Rochester when St. John is proposing spurs Jane to the next stage of her journey.

St. John also serves as a foil to Jane's other male cousin, John Reed. Their similarity of name heightens the difference between the two: St. John's self-restraint and desire to dedicate his life to God contrast with the drunken, dissolute, debt-ridden John, who commits suicide.

Diana and Mary Rivers

Diana and Mary are Jane's cousins, sisters to St. John. Like Jane, they must work as governesses to support themselves. Diana supports Jane after St. John proposes to her. Both sisters are positive role models for Jane, being intelligent, kind and independent. They share an emotional and intellectual connection. The sisters serve as foils to Eliza and Georgiana Reed. They also create a loving and welcoming home on terms of equality with Jane, which again contrasts with that of the Reed family.

The name Diana means 'heavenly' and 'divine' while the name Mary is an Egyptian name meaning 'beloved' and is also associated with Mary, mother of Jesus. Both names therefore connote religion and innate goodness.

Rosamond Oliver

Rosamond is the beautiful daughter of Mr. Oliver, the richest man in Morton. She has furnished the cottage that is attached to the school, and she pays for the education and clothing of an orphan from the workhouse. She loves St. John in vain, so becomes engaged to another man called Mr. Granby.

Useful Quotations

The quotations that follow are useful because they link to a variety of characters, themes, contextual elements, language and structural features. You are not expected to memorise all of them, so highlight half a dozen or so that you feel you can memorise easily and just read the others.

The examiner is looking for an ability to use short quotations worked into your own sentences and to make relevant textual references. A relevant textual reference means to paraphrase a quotation if you cannot remember the exact words. Both sorts of comment should be worked into the flow of your own sentences for maximum impact.

Chapter

1. **Quote:** Gateshead: 'cold winter wind' and 'penetrating' rain

    Relevance: Jane's treatment from Reeds. Family. Pathetic fallacy.

1. **Quote:** John Reed to Jane: 'you ought to beg, and not to live here with gentlemen's children like us'.

    Relevance: Reeds. Jane. Social class. Money. Family.

2. **Quote:** Bessie to Jane: 'if she were to turn you off, you would have to go to the poorhouse'

    Relevance: Mrs Reed. Social Hierarchy. Context. Family.

3. **Quote:** Miss Abbot says she might feel sorry for Jane if she were a 'nice, pretty child' but calls her a 'little toad'.

    Relevance: Jane. Society's view of female looks. Language analysis.

6. **Quotes:** Jane to Helen Burns: 'When we are struck at without a reason, we should strike back again very hard'. Helen Burns to Jane: 'Love your enemies; bless them that curse you'.

    Relevance: Jane and Helen Burns—foils. Passion vs. restraint. Religion to instruct/help.

7. **Quotes:** Mr Brocklehurst says 'that girl's hair must be cut off entirely'. Yet Mr Brocklehurst's daughters have 'elaborately curled' hair and his wife 'a false front of French curls'.

    Relevance: Mr Brocklehurst. Hypocrisy. Female appearances. Gender relations. Social status.

10. **Quote:** Bessie visits Jane before she leaves Lowood and says: 'The Miss Reeds could not play as well!'

Relevance: Dialogue helps the reader to measure Jane's accomplishments. Eliza and Georgiana Reed as foils to Jane. Education. Social class. Irony (Reeds have more money to spend on education).

11. **Quote:** Mrs Fairfax to Jane: 'I am so glad you are come' - 'they are only servants, and one can't converse with them on terms of equality'

    Relevance: Mrs Fairfax. Social hierarchy. Warm welcome = family/home.

11. **Quote:** 'It was a curious laugh; distinct, formal, mirthless'

    Relevance: Bertha Rochester. Gothic horror. Context. Structure (suspense). Language analysis (rule of three adjectives)

12. **Quote:** 'women feel just as men feel… they suffer from too rigid a restraint, too absolute a stagnation, precisely as men would suffer'

    Relevance: Women. Gender relations. Patriarchal context. Language & irony: (1) Jane is metaphorically imprisoned at Thornfield before arrival of Mr Rochester. (2) Bertha is physically imprisoned.

13. **Quote:** Mr Rochester says that Jane has 'the look of another world'. He adds that when he first saw her, he thought 'of fairy tales'. He wonders if she 'bewitched' his horse.

    Relevance: Jane. Mr Rochester. Supernatural. Gender relations. Spiritual connection.

14. **Quote:** Adèle: 'Ma boîte! ma boîte!' Mr Rochester: 'you genuine daughter of Paris'

    Relevance: Adèle. Mr Rochester. Attitudes to foreigners. Gender. Use of French dialogue to emphasise foreignness.

16. **Quote:** 'Portrait of a Governess, disconnected, poor, and plain' - 'Blanche, an accomplished lady of rank'

    Relevance: Jane's pictures. Jane and Blanche as foils. Social hierarchy. Money. Women's appearances.

17. **Quote:** Blanche about governesses: 'half of them detestable and the rest ridiculous'

    Relevance: Social hierarchy. Irony of Blanche's name.

18. **Quote:** Jane observes Blanche and Mr Rochester in the game of charades: 'pantomime of a marriage'

    Relevance: Jane. Blanche. Mr Rochester. Marriage. Gender relations. Foreshadows attempted bigamous sham marriage. Context: (1) answer is first part of Bridewell—symbolism of Bridewell prison. (2) divorce laws. Symbolises Mr Rochester's marriage.

18. **Quote:** Jane observes Mr Rochester and Blanche: 'I saw he was going to marry her' - 'her rank and connections suited him' - 'she could not charm him'

   Relevance: Blanche and Jane as foils. Rational marriage vs. compatibility. Social status. Money. Supernatural imagery. Use if italics.

20. **Quote:** Mr Mason to Mr Rochester in front of Jane: 'She bit me' - 'She sucked the blood: she said she'd drain my heart'

   Relevance: Gothic horror ('Vampyre' imagery). Gender relations. Context.

20. **Quote:** Mr Rochester: 'You are my little friend, are you not?' Jane: 'I like to serve you, sir, and to obey you in all that is right.'

   Relevance: Mr Rochester. Jane. Gender relations. Social hierarchy. Language: contrasts.

23. **Quote:** The sky is 'burning with the light of red jewel and furnace flame at one point'.

   Relevance: Gender relations. Marriage. Spiritual equality. Pathetic fallacy—divine disapproval. Passion.

23. **Quote:** Jane: 'Your bride stands between us.' Mr Rochester: 'my equal is here, and my likeness. Jane, will you marry me?'

   Relevance: Jane. Mr Rochester. Marriage. Irony: Jane talks about Blanche but Bertha stands between them. Direct, plain language. Social status. Spiritual equality.

24. **Quote:** Mr Rochester: 'I will myself put the diamond chain round your neck'. Jane: 'I am your plain, Quakerish governess'.

   Relevance: Mr Rochester. Jane. Marriage and context.

25. **Quote:** Jane to Mr Rochester after seeing Bertha, mistakes her for a 'Vampyre'.

   Relevance: Supernatural. Gothic horror. Structure: adds more suspense because the older Jane who is narrating the story deliberately withholds the fact that it is Bertha. Gender relations. Language: Bertha did bite her brother, Mr Mason, and she metaphorically drains the life out of Mr Rochester.

25. **Quote:** Jane to Mr Rochester about Bertha: 'a discoloured face—it was a savage face'

   Relevance: Foils. Attitudes to foreigners.

25. **Quote:** 'the veil, torn from top to bottom in two halves!'

Relevance: Bertha Rochester. Jane. Marriage. Unrestrained passion. Symbolism. Foreshadowing.

25. **Quote:** 'the great horse-chestnut at the bottom of the orchard had been struck by lightning in the night, and half of it split away'

    Relevance: Pathetic fallacy. Marriage. Divine retribution. Foreshadowing.

26. **Quote:** After the attempted marriage, Mr Rochester shows everyone Bertha: 'Compare these clear eyes with the red balls yonder—this face with that mask—this form with that bulk'

    Relevance: Bertha and Jane as foils. Marriage/context of divorce. Language contrasts.

26. **Quote:** 'it snatched and growled like some strange wild animal'

    Relevance: Jane about Bertha Rochester—women are foils. Marriage context. Attitude to foreigners. Passion versus restraint.

27. **Quote:** Mr Rochester is in a 'fury' and he seems to 'devour' Jane with his 'flaming glance'

    Relevance: Mr Rochester. Uncontrolled passion. Heat imagery.

27. **Quote:** Jane rejects Mr Rochester's suggestion to become his mistress: 'I will respect myself. I will keep the law given by God'

    Relevance: Jane. Mr Rochester. Passion vs. restraint. Gender relations. Religion.

30. **Quote:** At Moor House: 'Diana offered to teach me German. I liked to learn of her'

    Relevance: Jane. Diana Rivers. Structure: (1) Like a child at Lowood, Jane is taking the role of a pupil. (2) Diana is a female role model, just like Miss Temple and Helen Burns. Education: (1) Jane's recovery process. (2) More skills to earn more money. Equal social status.

31. **Quote:** When taking up position of school mistress in Morton: 'the germs of native excellence, refinement, intelligence, kind feeling, are as likely to exist in their hearts as in those of the best-born' - 'I felt degraded'

    Relevance: Jane. Education. Social Class. Irony: The Reeds and Blanche do not have these attributes. Language: Jane's conflicting feelings.

32. **Quote:** St. John tells Jane: 'I love Rosamond Oliver so wildly', adding 'she would not make me a good wife'

    Relevance: Marriage. Passion vs. restraint. St. John is a foil to Jane and Mr Rochester's ideas about marrying for love.

32. **Quotes:** St. John describes himself as a 'cold hard man'. Imagery of coldness, used multiple times in the novel: 'ice' – 'frozen sea' – 'avalanche' -'marble'

   Relevance: St. John, cold, hard imagery.

33. **Quotes:** St. John: 'I am cold: no fervour infects me'

34. Jane about St. John: 'no more of a husband's heart for me than that frowning giant of a rock' - 'He prizes me as a soldier would a good weapon'

   Relevance: St. John (foil to Mr Rochester). Passion vs. restraint. Rational marriage. Attitudes to women. Religion. Cold, hard imagery. War imagery.

34. **Quote:** 'I claim you - not for my pleasure, but for my Sovereign's service'

   Relevance: St. John to Jane. Gender relations. Marriage and context. Religion. Passion vs. restraint.

34. **Quote:** Jane contemplating marriage to St. John: 'always restrained, and always checked—forced to keep the fire of my nature continually low'

   Relevance: Jane. St. John. Passion vs. restraint. Marriage and context.

35. **Quote:** 'I never had a home, I never had brothers or sisters; I must and will have them now'

   Relevance: Jane. Rivers family (foils to Jane's Reed cousins). Home/family. Passion.

35. **Quote:** When St. John proposes to Jane, she has a psychic or spiritual connection with Mr Rochester and hears his voice: 'it spoke in pain and woe, wildly, eerily, urgently'

   Relevance: Jane. Mr Rochester. Gender relations. Supernatural—psychic connection. Religion. Language analysis: list of adverbs.

38. **Quote:** 'Reader, I married him'

   Relevance: Jane about Mr Rochester. Marriage. Gender roles and language: active rather than passive sentence, which was shocking in context.

Example GCSE Exam Responses

Example Response 1

Explore how Brontë presents Jane's feelings of being an outsider:

- **In this extract**
- **And elsewhere in the novel**

> There was no possibility of taking a walk that day. We had been wandering, indeed, in the leafless shrubbery an hour in the morning; but since dinner (Mrs. Reed, when there was no company, dined early) the cold winter wind had brought with it clouds so sombre, and a rain so penetrating, that further out-door exercise was now out of the question.
>
> I was glad of it: I never liked long walks, especially on chilly afternoons: dreadful to me was the coming home in the raw twilight, with nipped fingers and toes, and a heart saddened by the chidings of Bessie, the nurse, and humbled by the consciousness of my physical inferiority to Eliza, John, and Georgiana Reed.
>
> The said Eliza, John, and Georgiana were now clustered round their mama in the drawing-room: she lay reclined on a sofa by the fireside, and with her darlings about her (for the time neither quarrelling nor crying) looked perfectly happy. Me, she had dispensed from joining the group; saying, "She regretted to be under the necessity of keeping me at a distance; but that until she heard from Bessie, and could discover by her own observation, that I was endeavouring in good earnest to acquire a more sociable and childlike disposition, a more attractive and sprightly manner—something lighter, franker, more natural, as it were—she really must exclude me from privileges intended only for contented, happy, little children."
>
> "What does Bessie say I have done?" I asked.
>
> "Jane, I don't like cavillers or questioners; besides, there is something truly forbidding in a child taking up her elders in that manner. Be seated somewhere; and until you can speak pleasantly, remain silent."

The older Jane narrates the story in the first person and reflects on the younger Jane feeling an outsider. She guides our responses through sentence length and pathetic fallacy. The declarative 'There was no possibility of taking a walk that day' is short for emphasis and encourages the reader to believe that Jane is disappointed about not going on a walk. The longer second sentence is a detailed description of the weather and appears to be an explanation for why she cannot go on a walk. Through pathetic fallacy, we see sensory words with 'cold winter wind' and 'penetrating' – 'rain', which might symbolise the dispassionate, harsh, bullying treatment that Jane receives from the Reeds. The use of this moment therefore introduces Jane's feelings of being an outsider because the pathetic fallacy creates a sense of unease and introduces a tone of hostility.

The abrupt 'I was glad of it' at the start of the next paragraph is a shock, as the reader realises that Jane is not disappointed. It therefore introduces a sense of independence as she asserts her thoughts. This prepares us for her rebellious behaviour (which is how she copes with being an outsider) later in the chapter.

Brontë uses dialogue to emphasise Jane's feelings of being an outsider. The older Jane chooses to report Mrs Reed's very formal speech ('She regretted to be under the necessity of keeping me at a distance…'), which is an unusual way to speak to a young relation. This illustrates that Mrs Reed does not, in her formal politeness, love or feel empathy for Jane. Moreover, it shows the reader that Jane's feelings of being an outsider are valid because she is being physically kept at a distance from the family.

Through reporting Mrs Reed's words, the reader learns that Jane is made to feel isolated because she does not conform to the norms of contemporary attitudes to young girls: Mrs Reed expects a 'more sociable and childlike disposition, a more attractive and sprightly manner—something lighter, franker, more natural'. Jane is therefore made to feel like an outsider because young girls at that time were expected to be pleasing. The reader therefore learns that Jane is not a conventional protagonist; this adds realism to her character, and the reader is encouraged to empathise with her feelings of being an outsider.

Jane's response ('What does Bessie say I have done?') is couched in very simple language spoken by a child, which contrasts with Mrs Reed's verbose formal speech. Jane, as a female child, is expected to be passive. Instead, she challenges her situation with an interrogative. Mrs Reed tells her off for 'taking up her elders' and the use of this moment foreshadows her fighting back against John Reed in 'fury' and 'passion'. Jane therefore rejects contemporary gender roles, which adds to her feelings of isolation.

Perhaps Jane's feelings of being an outsider in the Reed family are a metaphor for the situation of girls at that time. Living restricted lives, they did not enjoy the same education as boys or have the same career opportunities. When the novel was published, it was unusual to write from the point of view of a female, especially a female child. By choosing this narrative device, Brontë challenges the tradition of gender hierarchy. This, combined with her beliefs about how women were restricted in Victorian society, indicates that she believed a girl's thoughts and feelings were of equal importance to a man's. Furthermore, by including Jane's feelings about being an outsider as a child, the reader is invited to draw comparisons between her as a young child and between later in the novel when she is a woman. Employing the form of a Bildungsroman therefore illustrates Jane's emotional journey, which is not only physical but also spiritual. This provides Brontë's female readers with the opportunity to examine societal expectations of female roles.

***

In the rest of the novel, Jane's feelings of being an outsider are perhaps strongest at the start of the Moor House chapters when she becomes a beggar. We see through the words and actions of the characters how beggars of the time may have been treated. At one point, Jane begs for and receives some hardened porridge that was destined for pigs. Spoilt porridge symbolises the lowest level of deprivation, humiliation and hopelessness possible. At Lowood, the pupils are served 'burnt porridge', which is described as so inedible that 'famine itself soon sickens over it'. The personification of 'famine' emphasises how disgusting the food is. When Jane becomes a beggar, she eats a 'stiffened mould' of porridge and is so grateful that she devours it 'ravenously', contrasting with her rejection of the burnt porridge as a child. This symbolises the depths to which she has been reduced as an outsider.

Even as a beggar, her feelings of being an outsider are heightened through other people's reactions to her: 'an ordinary beggar is frequently an object of suspicion; a well-dressed beggar inevitably so'. She is therefore neither a conventional beggar nor a rich lady. Appearance can also be misinterpreted, as we see when the servant Hannah turns Jane away from Moor House: 'You are not what you ought to be, or you wouldn't make such a noise'. This comment implies that Jane is a prostitute, which is ironic, considering her modest character and preference for wearing 'Quakerish' clothes. Perhaps Brontë wants to convey a moral message to the Victorian public about the importance of helping the poor, regardless of their status and appearance. As the daughter of a clergyman, she would have been keenly aware of the morality of behaving like a good Christian and helping outsiders.

Example Response 2

Explore how Brontë uses setting to develop atmosphere:

- **In this extract**
- **And elsewhere in the novel**

> A breakfast-room adjoined the drawing-room, I slipped in there. It contained a bookcase: I soon possessed myself of a volume, taking care that it should be one stored with pictures. I mounted into the window-seat: gathering up my feet, I sat cross-legged, like a Turk; and, having drawn the red moreen curtain nearly close, I was shrined in double retirement.
>
> Folds of scarlet drapery shut in my view to the right hand; to the left were the clear panes of glass, protecting, but not separating me from the drear November day. At intervals, while turning over the leaves of my book, I studied the aspect of that winter afternoon. Afar, it offered a pale blank of mist and cloud; near a scene of wet lawn and storm-beat shrub, with ceaseless rain sweeping away wildly before a long and lamentable blast.

The setting creates a feeling of loneliness in the first paragraph with the repetition of the pronoun 'I', which is used five times to emphasise that Jane is in a separate room to the Reed family. However, Brontë's of choice of nouns implies Jane's self-reliance: 'bookcase' – 'volume' – 'pictures' – 'window-seat' and 'retirement' imply that she can adapt to her environment by finding solace in books. The simile 'like a Turk' provides evidence of her education (as does the fact that she knows the name of the material 'moreen') and that she is using her imagination as a coping strategy.

In the second paragraph, the setting contains vivid visual imagery of the 'red' or 'scarlet' of the curtains which juxtaposes with the pale colours outside the room to develop atmosphere. The colour red usually signifies blood or danger, which reminds us that the Reed home is not a comfortable place for her. Another interpretation is that the 'scarlet drapery' is comforting womb-like imagery, which suggests that, like an unborn baby, Jane has not yet entered the world and is perhaps reluctant to do so. The pathetic fallacy and colourless imagery of the 'pale blank of mist and cloud' contrasts with the 'scarlet' and suggests a clash between Jane and her environment. She cannot at this stage see a way out of her situation, just as it is not possible to see through mist. The narrative structure unravels to reveal violent weather imagery at the end of the second paragraph. The imagery of the 'storm-beat shrub, with ceaseless rain' and the use of the onomatopoeia 'blast' combine to symbolise that Jane is vulnerable and at the mercy of her family. This imagery foreshadows aunt's abuse of her when she locks Jane in the 'red-room', providing more evidence of the unsettling atmosphere in the house.

This womb imagery contrasts with the horror of the 'red-room' at the end of the chapter when Jane is isolated and surrounded by the colour 'red'. The gothic use of red becomes hellish and, like a gothic heroine, Jane faints because of the overwhelming horror of seeing the ghostly light. Narrated in the first person, the older Jane reflects on her life as a child and guides the reader's response. This is important for later in the novel where we see a completely different reaction to her setting. For example, Mr Rochester asks Jane if she turns 'sick at the sight of blood' in chapter 20 because a contemporary stereotype was that women were so fragile and emotional that they would faint at the sight of blood. By helping Mr Rochester and not fainting, we can measure how Jane, who does not faint, is taking an active male role and mastering her response to a challenging setting by staunching Mr Mason's blood. This contrasts with her stereotypically passive female response of earlier fainting in the red-room, which is the colour of blood. Through Jane's responses to her setting, we therefore have a yardstick by which to measure her development, and Brontë challenges contemporary beliefs about women being weak.

**

Elsewhere in the novel, we see the influences of the gothic genre with the atmospheric setting of Jane's journey to Thornfield Hall through the 'misty' night. She hears the 'tolling' bell as they pass the church, and the entrance gates of Thornfield Hall 'clash' behind them. The 'dark' building is lit by 'candlelight'. These atmospheric words foreshadow elements of Jane's life. Like the mist outside the breakfast-room window at Gateshead, the mist on the journey to Thornfield Hall foreshadows Jane's future inability to see her situation clearly, as secrets will be hidden from her; bells usually toll at funerals, so the 'tolling' church bell could foreshadow the death of her hopes and expectations as well as the later death of Bertha Rochester; the 'clash' of the gates behind her might symbolise Bertha's imprisonment and Jane's future concerns about losing her identity in marriage; the 'dark' building could represent hidden secrets; and 'candlelight' has associations with Bertha's future attempts to burn down Thornfield, but might also remind the reader that, at Thornfield, Jane's passion and love for Mr Rochester will burn brightly. The gothic imagery therefore introduces the setting, creates a sense of mystery and unease, and develops the idea of events being controlled by the supernatural.

Example Response 3

In this extract, the servants Bessie and Miss Abbot, under orders from Mrs Reed, lock Jane in the red-room. Explore how Brontë presents social hierarchy:

- **In this extract**
- **And elsewhere in the novel**

> Bessie answered not; but ere long, addressing me, she said—"You ought to be aware, Miss, that you are under obligations to Mrs. Reed: she keeps you: if she were to turn you off, you would have to go to the poorhouse."
>
> I had nothing to say to these words: they were not new to me: my very first recollections of existence included hints of the same kind. This reproach of my dependence had become a vague sing-song in my ear: very painful and crushing, but only half intelligible. Miss Abbot joined in—
>
> "And you ought not to think yourself on an equality with the Misses Reed and Master Reed, because Missis kindly allows you to be brought up with them. They will have a great deal of money, and you will have none: it is your place to be humble, and to try to make yourself agreeable to them."
>
> "What we tell you is for your good," added Bessie, in no harsh voice, "you should try to be useful and pleasant, then, perhaps, you would have a home here; but if you become passionate and rude, Missis will send you away, I am sure."
>
> "Besides," said Miss Abbot, "God will punish her: He might strike her dead in the midst of her tantrums, and then where would she go? Come, Bessie, we will leave her: I wouldn't have her heart for anything. Say your prayers, Miss Eyre, when you are by yourself; for if you don't repent, something bad might be permitted to come down the chimney and fetch you away."
>
> They went, shutting the door, and locking it behind them.

The use of this scene highlights the theme of social hierarchy and Jane's vulnerability as a dependent orphan living at Gateshead. The two servants contrast in their attitude to Jane. The harsh Miss Abbot tells Jane that she is 'less than a servant' because she does nothing to support herself, and the kinder Bessie, who speaks 'in no harsh voice', reminds Jane that she is 'under obligations to Mrs Reed: she keeps you: if she were to turn you off, you would have to go to the Poorhouse'. This information is shocking to the reader, who would not expect a rich relation to treat a dependent child in such a way. The servants therefore serve to emphasise Jane's vulnerability in the house. Perhaps the harshness and kindness of the women is a metaphor for the contrasting attitudes to the poor in Victorian society.

Brontë employs dialogue to emphasise Jane's position in a class-ridden society. Both servants use judgemental language and imperatives, repeating 'you ought to'. Miss Abbot takes this to more of an extreme by using hyperbole ('God might strike her dead' and 'something bad might be permitted to come down the chimney and fetch you away') to frighten her into submission. Bessie's more sympathetic approach can be shown by the increased use of commas in her complex sentences to soften what she is saying ('then, perhaps, you would have a home here' and 'if you become passionate and rude, Missis will send you away, I am sure'. Her use of 'perhaps', 'if' and the final 'I am sure' add to the more sympathetic tone. Despite their contrasting ways of emphasising Jane's position to her, to both women, she is a penniless orphan, and this defines her status. Jane's social status in the eyes of society is not quite so easy to define, however. She cannot claim the same social status as her rich family, yet, being waited on in the house, she is above a servant, despite what they say.

Brontë emphasises this moment as a learning point for Jane by her reactions to the servants: the older Jane, who is narrating the story, employs a reflective tone and guides our responses using time. We have the distant past ('my very first recollections of existence included hints of the same kind') and the present: 'This reproach of my dependence had become a vague sing-song in my ear: very painful and crushing, but only half intelligible'. The juxtaposition of 'vague sing-song' and 'only half intelligible' with the adjectives 'very painful and crushing' imply that she had not been fully aware of why the Reeds, who should be protecting her, are hurting her. The use of this moment with the servants' plain-speaking direct speech therefore leaves no room for doubt about Jane's awareness of her position in the social hierarchy from this moment onwards.

***

Elsewhere in the novel, Brontë uses contrast to show that wealth and status are not always a good indication of character. For example, when Bessie visits Jane at Lowood (chapter 10), she says that Jane looks 'like a lady' and is 'charmed' when Jane plays the piano, draws and speaks French better than her cousins Georgiana and Eliza Reed. John Reed, we also learn, is now 'a dissipated young man'. Jane looks and behaves more like a member of the upper class than her cousins, so it is ironic that their social status is higher. Through the contrast between Jane and her Reed cousins, Brontë encourages the reader to judge people by the example they set rather than by the class that they are born to.

Elsewhere in the novel, Jane's position in the social hierarchy isolates her to the point of social exclusion. As a governess, she is of a higher class than the servants but of a lower class than Mr Rochester and his guests. (Mrs Fairfax is of a similar status to Jane, but she is not Jane's intellectual equal.) Because she is a governess, Jane is socially excluded by Mr Rochester's guests. Foremost among these is Jane's foil, Blanche, 'the very type of majesty'. The use of 'majesty' suggests that Jane believes her to be at the top of the social hierarchy, which contrasts with Jane's lower social status. Despite knowing that Jane can hear her, Blanche calls governesses 'detestable' and 'ridiculous'. These adjectives reveal a supercilious attitude and, by sneering at governesses in front of a governess, Jane encourages the reader to judge the upper classes and to question the contemporary assumption that upper-class people are morally superior people.

Printed in Great Britain
by Amazon

83306606R00056